# The Time of Your Life

## Mark Porter

While this book is designed for the reader's personal enjoyment and profit, it is also intended for group study. A Leader's Guide with Victor Multiuse Transparency Masters is available from your local bookstore or from the publisher.

**VICTOR BOOKS** a division of SP Publications, Inc.

WHEATON. ILLINOIS 60187

*Offices also in*
Whitby, Ontario, Canada
Amersham-on-the-Hill, Bucks, England

Recommended Dewey Decimal Classification: 248.4
  Suggested Subject Headings: TIME EFFICIENCY, CHRISTIAN LIFE.

Library of Congress Catalog Card Number: 82-61038
ISBN: 88207-387-7

# Contents

To my wife, Carol, and our two sons,
Greg and Tim, whose love, patience, and
encouragement during the writing of this
book were more than I could ask

... and to my typist, Patt Greig,
whose perseverance and labor
of love are unrivaled.

# Preface

Are you busier than ever, but accomplishing less? Has the joy of the Lord been replaced by a driven feeling? Do you complain to God about not having enough time?

This was the story of my life: never enough time, chronically caught in the scurry syndrome. My wife felt I had taken on too many responsibilities: a management post in a high-technology company, teaching elder and director of family ministries at church, a husband and father. I could spend fulltime in any of these areas. Each competed for my time.

I have discovered there is enough time! Friends ask how I do it all. There is *more* than enough time to do what God wants us to do.

At the end of three-and-a-half years of ministry, Jesus reported to His Father, "I have finished the work which Thou gavest Me to do" (John 17:4, KJV). He accomplished more in that short span than anyone has accomplished in a lifetime, yet we never see Him in a frenzy to get things done. Nor was He too busy to interrupt His plans for others. Yet He was in control of His time and His life. He had a peace and a calmness which is not suggested in most time-management books. He wants us to have this too. "Peace I leave with you, My peace I give unto you" (John 14:27, KJV).

The goal of this book is not to make you a *time nut*, but to help you to accomplish all that God wants you to do—with peace.

I originally developed the principles presented here for use in time-management seminars. Enthusiastic participants in these seminars suggested I put these principles in print. I am convinced that time management is one of the most important skills we can learn. It makes us more valuable to the Lord, to the organizations we serve, and to ourselves.

*Mark Porter*

# 1
# Activity vs Accomplishment

I became interested in time management while a freshman at the Massachusetts Institute of Technology. I had come to M.I.T. as valedictorian of my high school class and expected to make straight A's. I discovered every other M.I.T. student had been a valedictorian too. Competition was stiff, and I was on the way to flunking.

I cut out all extracurricular activities and tried to get by on five hours of sleep, but my grades only got worse.

I didn't pray much when times were good, but prayer took on new importance. Still my grades got worse. "What good is God, if He's not here when I need Him?" I cried.

I began to read the Bible to find out whether I knew how to pray. I discovered that, though I had joined the church at age 10, I was not a Christian. I learned that I was a sinner and needed to be forgiven and brought into a right relationship with God through Jesus Christ. When I read "Seek ye first the kingdom of God and His righteousness; and all these things shall be added unto you" (Matt. 6:33, KJV) the issue became clear to me. God was not first in my life. Grades were my god and success was my idol.

After a struggle of several weeks, I turned over management of my life to Jesus Christ. I determined to seek first the kingdom of God and His righteousness. My days began with Bible reading and prayer. I attended the dormitory Bible study and church on Sundays. I wrote letters to make restitution and to ask forgiveness.

Meanwhile, I was seriously seeking God's will for my life. I kept plugging away at my studies, wondering how God would lead. Since I expected to flunk, I thought God might send me to Bible school.

To my amazement, the next round of exams turned up with A's and B's instead of D's and F's. I was studying less; I had other priorities. What had happened? Then I remembered the verse: "Seek ye first the kingdom of God and His righteousness; and all these things will be added unto you." God had spoken through His Word and through circumstances: "Mark, M.I.T. is where I wanted you all along, but your priorities were messed up. Put Me first, and I will bless you." Without the Lord, my labor was in vain; I could accomplish nothing of real value. C. S. Lewis wrote, "Aim at heaven and you will get earth thrown in. Aim at earth and you will get neither."

This principle appears over and over in the Old and New Testaments. "Unless the Lord builds the house, they labor in vain who build it; unless the Lord guards the city, the watchman keeps awake in vain. It is vain for you to rise up early, to retire late, to eat the bread of painful labors; for He gives to His beloved even in his sleep" (Ps. 127:1-2). Labor is in vain unless the Lord is in it—unless the laborer knows the Lord as "his beloved."

The Book of Haggai reminds us of the futility of any endeavor which neglects God. "You have sown much, and harvested little; you eat, but you never have enough; you drink, but you never have your fill; you clothe yourselves, but no one is warm; and he who earns wages, earns wages to put them into a bag with holes. Why? says the Lord of hosts. Because of My house that lies in ruins, while you busy yourselves each with his own house" (1:6, 9, RSV). When the people reordered their priorities and put God first, they began to prosper and the Lord said, "From this day on I will bless you" (2:19, RSV).

Peter and his partners had fished all night and caught nothing. When Jesus taught from their boat, He urged them to let down their nets again. Peter probably wondered what a carpenter knew about fishing and replied, "Master, we worked hard all night and caught nothing, but at Your bidding I will let down the nets"

(Luke 5:5). No sooner had he obeyed than the nets began to break under the load of fish. Two boats were not enough to hold the catch.

My first rule for successful time managment, then, is: "Seek ye first the kingdom of God and His righteousness; and all these things shall be added unto you" (Matt. 6:33, KJV). You can work hard at time management, but unless God is number one, you will be spinning your wheels.

## Mounting up with Eagles' Wings

There are projects for which we feel totally incapable. We may feel drained of energy. We know we cannot attain the heights demanded of us, nor can we keep up the pace.

In Isaiah we read that if we "wait for the Lord" we will "mount up with wings like eagles" (Isa. 40:31, RSV). Eagles fly higher than any bird; the eagle's wingspan (up to 7 feet) allows it to glide effortlessly to altitudes of over 2,400 feet. A great bald eagle was once clocked at speeds in excess of 150 miles per hour. The eagle's wings are powerful—capable of carrying objects which approach its own body weight (up to 12 pounds). Eagles have been known to transport small lambs a distance of several miles.

We have the promise of God-given strength that enables us to carry on while others grow weary or faint. We don't achieve this by trying harder. It is "not I, but Christ."

When Martin Luther entered a particularly busy time in his life, he increased his prayertime. He explained to a friend, "I have so much business I cannot get along without spending three hours daily in prayer. If I fail to spend three hours in prayer each morning, the devil gets the victory through the day."

Most people try to solve their time-management problems by putting in more time, but working longer hours does not always result in more accomplished. Good time management is doing more in the time allotted—maximizing output for a given input. It is working smarter, not harder. To do this, we need the Lord's wisdom and strength.

There is a tendency in our society to be more concerned with input than output. Employees are seldom remunerated on the basis of piecework; they receive an hourly wage instead. Even salesmen, who traditionally have been paid on a commission basis, now are paid a salary. Too often executives are evaluated on how busy they are. The manager with a crowded schedule, a bulging briefcase, and jangled nerves is rated high. In reality, he may have lost sight of his prioritites.

Even in the ministry we concentrate on input rather than output, because results are difficult to measure. Realizing God values quality more than quantity, we are uncomfortable keeping track of attendance records. We convince ourselves we are doing a good job by the number of hours (blood, sweat, and tears) we put in. Meanwhile our spiritual lives are at low ebb because of overwork. We no longer take time to "wait for the Lord."

Poor time management is seen in two extremes: the lazy person who loathes work and the workaholic who overworks. The irony is that people concerned about better managing their time usually have the latter problem. If you're reading this book, you're probably already doing more than you should. That's why you need to learn to work smarter—not harder.

## Workaholics Anonymous

If you feel driven and exhausted most of the time, you may be a workaholic. Here's a checklist:

- You're never too busy to stop and talk about how busy you are.
- When someone talks to you for over five minutes, you look at your watch.
- You seldom relax or play because there is always another project to be done.
- You are unable to say *no* when you are asked to do something.
- You set unrealistic goals for yourself.
- You are irritable, disillusioned with people, and depressed much of the time.
- Your spouse asks if you have given him or her up for Lent; and your son or daughter thinks an appointment is needed to talk with you.

- You never go on vacation because you believe things will fall apart while you're away.
- If you do go on vacation, you take more than one book for each day you will be away.
- You try to be everywhere at once.

Too much busyness often indicates unsurrendered areas in our lives. For example, we may find it difficult to say *no* because we care too much about what people think and not enough about the Lord's priorities for our lives.

Our heavenly Father never gives us more than we can do. Men will! We may even assign ourselves an overload, but the Lord will not. He is distressed when we are overloaded. "Come unto Me, all ye that labor and are heavy laden, and I will give you rest. Take My yoke upon you, and learn of Me ... for My yoke is easy, and My burden is light" (Matt. 11:28-30, KJV). Compulsive overwork usually means we're taking on more than His yoke; we're out of step—getting ahead of the Lord—and unwilling to wait for Him.

Overwork is also harmful to interpersonal relationships. Workaholics are irritable, fussy, and distant. They are to time what Scrooge was to money. Overwork may even be a subconscious excuse for avoiding close personal relationships.

Workaholics are prime candidates for burnout. Remember Joe? He did everything! He was active in evangelism and visitation. He led a small fellowship group. He taught a Sunday School class. He discipled younger Christians. Then Joe began to relinquish these responsibilities. Christian friends tried to exhort him, but only succeeded in driving him further away. Today Joe doesn't attend church anywhere. What happened? He is a victim of church burnout.

Dr. Herbert J. Freudenberger, a New York psychoanalyst, has written a book called *Burnout: The High Cost of High Achievement*. He defines a burnout as "someone in a state of fatigue or frustration brought about by devotion to a cause, a way of life, or relationship that failed to produce the expected reward" (Doubleday, p. 13).

*Burnout* is not to be confused with *rustout*, suffered by those who are inactive and uninvolved. Burnout casualties are dynamic, goal-oriented, high achievers.

Nor should burnout be confused with *copout*. Demas forsook Paul because Demas loved the world—a *copout* but not a *burnout*.

Zealous Christians are particularly susceptible to burnout because they have idealistic aspirations and high expectations. We can prevent burnout by setting realistic goals and recognizing our limitations. Workaholics need to build leisure into their schedules—even if it means forcing themselves to play racquetball once a week or to pursue a new hobby.

## Come Apart and Rest—or Come Apart

The disciples had returned from an exhausting preaching tour, and Jesus urged them to come apart from the crowds to a quiet place and rest (Mark 6:30-32). I believe the Lord is often more concerned about our need to rest than we are. He knows our limitations. "It is in vain that you rise up early, and go late to rest, eating the bread of anxious toil; for He gives to His beloved sleep" (Ps. 127:2, RSV). The Psalmist speaks of the Lord as a shepherd (Ps. 23) who, knowing what's best for His sheep, makes them lie down in green pastures to restore their souls. If we don't rest periodically, we will come apart.

In a survey of the couples who attend our monthly family enrichment time, 41 percent said the main causes of depression were fatigue and time pressure. Sixty percent ranked these among the top three causes. A. W. Tozer cautioned, "Whenever you feel out of it spiritually, before you go into hours of morbid introspection, the first thing you should do is get yourself 12 hours of sleep."

God emphasized the importance of rest by instituting the Sabbath, a day when work was forbidden. Not only did He recognize the restorative role of rest, He set apart the Sabbath as holy and higher than the other days of the week. Any view of leisure which makes it morally inferior to work is at odds with the concept of the Sabbath.

Man has created laws to insure proper rest. Long-distance truckers are not allowed to drive more than eight hours at a time. Airline flight crews are limited in how many hours they can fly at a time. Tired people make mistakes, and a mistake in driving or flying may be fatal.

Excellence does not come from tired people, mediocrity does. Professional athletes, musicians, surgeons, and others whose work demands excellence, build time into their schedules for rest, leisure, and change. This insures performance at peak efficiency.

Charles A. Garfield, a performance psychologist at the University of California Medical School (San Francisco) has spent 15 years interviewing 1,200 top performers in business, education, sports, and the arts. He was surprised to find that the best performers weren't workaholics. They took their vacations; they knew when to stop working; and they managed stress well (*Wall Street Journal*, Jan. 13, 1982).

Those who have studied creativity believe rest and play are essential ingredients in successful problem-solving. George Prince, in his book *The Practice of Creativity* (Collier, p. 20) has suggested that new ideas come primarily from the subconscious mind. As long as the conscious mind is actively working on a problem, it refuses to allow the subconscious to interrupt; therefore, in order to gain insights from the subconscious, we must divert the conscious mind to something else. For example, Thomas Edison practiced what he called half-working states to solve difficult problems. He would stretch out on the couch and daydream—picking up stray ideas as they popped into his mind. James D. Watson, along with Francis Crick, worked out one of biology's greatest riddles, the molecular structure of DNA, in similar fashion. Much to the dismay of his colleagues, Watson spent every afternoon on the tennis courts and many evenings at the movies. He felt it was necessary for ideas to incubate in his subconscious and then percolate into the conscious mind without undue pressure.

I think we've all experienced this in lesser or greater degree. Some of my best ideas have come to mind while I was jogging. The Spirit of God often speaks when I am least expecting it— while shaving, showering, or on awakening in the morning. The point is: We need relaxation and diversion to do our best work.

# 2

# Building for Eternity

Clarence Darrow (1857-1938) was perhaps the greatest criminal defense attorney in the history of the American bar. He was a master at manipulating juries, whether they were composed of homespun farmers or cultured aristocrats. He won freedom for the most hardened criminals. As a result, people were willing to pay huge sums for his services. He earned wealth, prestige, and power.

In his later years, Clarence Darrow became an unhappy man. One day he went to the chapel at the University of Chicago and heard a minister speak on the topic "All True Values and the Meaning of Life Are Found in Jesus Christ Alone." Afterward Darrow wrote to ask the minister to call on him. When the minister came Darrow told him, "I'm an old man, and I haven't found the way. Oh, in the eyes of the world, I'm a success. I chose criminal defense because I could make the most money and realize my potential. I had a way with men. I was so clever at it, I could get a fee of six figures for letting some rascal who was guilty go free. Now I'm old and wise enough to know that isn't life. I've been reading in the New Testament, and I came across a passage which is a fitting epitaph for my life. Jesus was preaching in the little boat by the seaside, and after His sermon, He told them to launch out and let down their nets for a great catch. The answer of one of those disciples is my life. 'Good teacher,' he said, 'we have toiled all night. . . .' " Tears were on the face of the old attorney. " 'We have toiled all night and taken *nothing*!' That is Clarence Darrow, and if you have anything to tell an old man who has failed, say on, sir, because I haven't found the meaning of life." (In this instance and throughout the book, the italics in Scripture references is added.)

Ernest Hemingway (1899-1961) went into creative writing as a young man. In 1953 he received the Pulitzer Prize for literature and in 1954, the Nobel Prize for literature. He had arrived! He had wealth, prestige, and fame. He could have had the chair of letters at any English-speaking university. He said, "When I arrive at the pinnacle of my desire and find that I have no adequacy within, I won't want to live any longer." In 1961 he took a gun and shot himself to death. His goals were empty! He had toiled all night and taken nothing.

Jesus spoke of a man who had accumulated much in the way of material wealth and who was looking forward to retirement when he could enjoy it. "But God said unto him, 'Thou fool, this night thy soul shall be required of thee: then whose shall those things be?' " (Luke 12:20, KJV)

## Rewards Are Earned

There is a misunderstanding among some Christians that all who trust in Christ will be ushered into heaven on an equal basis. Not so! "For we must all appear before the Judgment Seat of Christ; that each one may be recompensed for his deeds in the body, according to what he has done, whether good or bad" (2 Cor. 5:10). Some will receive rewards; others will not.

Paul speaks of each life as a building with Jesus Christ as the foundation. What's done in life for Christ is likened to gold, silver, or precious stones. What's done for ourselves is as wood, hay, or straw. The Master Himself will review what we have built. It will be tested by fire and what is of eternal value will remain, and for it we shall receive a reward. If it has no eternal value it will be consumed, and there will be no reward, though the life, because it stands on the foundation of Christ, will be saved "yet so as through fire" (1 Cor. 3:11-15).

Jesus went so far as to say we will give an account of every idle word we speak (Matt. 12:36). From that I conclude every moment of my life represents either gold, silver, and precious stones or wood, hay, and straw. I can't squander my time in vain pursuits and expect to receive a reward. I can't live a selfish life and expect to hear, "Well done, thou good and faithful servant."

Have you ever thought about what you will hear at the Judgment Seat of Christ? How will you account for your time? A survey shows the average Christian in the United States who lives 75 years, spends

| | |
|---|---|
| 23 of 75 years sleeping | (31% of our time) |
| 19 years working | (25%) |
| 9 years watching TV or other amusements | (12%) |
| 7½ years in dressing and personal care | (10%) |
| 6 years eating | ( 8%) |
| 6 years traveling | ( 8%) |
| ½ year worshiping and praying. | (0.7%) |

The frittering away of time in front of the idiot-box is equivalent to a little over 30 hours a week or 2 hours and 52 minutes a day. Assuming we get 8 hours of sleep a night with only 16 hours available to use every day, the figures are even more appalling. The average Christian spends 18 percent of his time awake in front of the set. That amounts to 65½ days (16-hour days) each year or 13½ years out of life—down the tube. How will we answer when the Lord asks, "What did you get out of 'Love Boat,' or 'The Odd Couple,' or 'The Johnny Carson Show'?" Our consciences must be our TV guide, and if necessary, we should cut the cord.

TV isn't the only "time bandit." Hours are wasted in other ways. Horace Mann lamented, "Lost yesterday, somewhere between sunrise and sunset, two golden hours, each set with sixty diamond minutes. No reward is offered, for they are gone forever."

We may regret years we sow to the flesh and reap corruption, but it is never too late to start sowing to the Spirit. When the people of Israel returned to the Lord and made a new beginning, God promised to restore to them the years that the locust had eaten ( Joel 2:25, KJV). More than anything else, God values willingness and determination to serve Him—even in the eleventh hour of life.

## We Are Responsible for Our Time

Jesus told a remarkable parable about a landowner who hired laborers for his vineyard (Matt. 20:1-16). He hired some at the beginning of the day, some at the third hour, and still others at the sixth, ninth, and eleventh hours. He paid them all the same! We cry "Unfair!" But the landowner fulfilled his agreement with those who worked all day, and he had no agreement with the others. They were willing to work, trusting that the landowner would treat them fairly at the end of the day. Those who began in the eleventh hour exercised the most faith. The short time for work did not promise much in remuneration, but they were willing to do what they could. The landowner valued their willingness to serve and gave them as much as those who labored the full day.

We have a similar situation in the Parable of the Talents (Matt. 25:14-30). The master gave one servant 5 talents, another 2 talents, and another, 1 talent. The first servant invested his 5 talents and increased them 100 percent to make 10. The second servant, who had 2 talents, increased them 100 percent to make 4. The master commended these two servants in exactly the same way: "Well done, thou good and faithful servant: thou hast been faithful over a few things; I will make thee ruler over many things. Enter thou into the joy of thy Lord" (Matt. 25:21, KJV).

Though each servant was given a different amount, the master followed the principle: "For unto whomsoever much is given, of him shall be much required" (Luke 12:48, KJV). We are responsible for the time we have been given.

The third servant did nothing with his talent. The master took his talent from him, called him an unprofitable servant, and cast him into outer darkness. Though we may have only a little time at our disposal (one lousy talent), we need to seize it and use it for the Lord.

"Behold, now is the accepted time; behold now is the day of salvation" (2 Cor. 6:2, KJV). "And that, knowing the time, that now it is high time to awake out of sleep: for now is our salvation nearer than when we believed. The night is far spent, the day is at hand: let us therefore cast off the works of darkness, and let us put on the armor of light" (Rom. 13:11-12, KJV). The lateness of the hour should motivate us to make the most of whatever time we have left.

If the bank credited your account every morning with $1,440 but wiped out any remaining balance at the end of the day, what would you do? You would draw $1,440 out each day so you could use it before you lost it. God credits our accounts at the beginning of every day with 1,440 minutes. Yesterday's balance is gone forever. Tomorrow's balance is not yet available. Today's time cannot be saved and stored for use tomorrow; it is like Israel's manna in the wilderness.

Daily rations are the same. God gives 1,440 minutes to the President of the United States, the chairman of General Motors, to Billy Graham, to you, and to me.

In the Parable of the Pounds (Luke 19), the Master entrusted each servant with 1 pound to invest until He returned. The ration was the same, but one servant made 10 pounds out of the 1. Another made 5 pounds. Their rewards were proportionate to what they accomplished. The first was given authority over 10 cities while the second was put over 5 cities. Still another servant did nothing with his pound and lost everything.

Both the Parable of the Pounds and the Parable of the Talents teach that our positions in heaven will be determined by how we use our time here.

## Instructions for Redeeming the Time

Time management is an essential part of building for eternity. In this book we will look at the example of the Lord Jesus in whose steps we are to follow. He was the perfect steward of time. At the end of life He could say that He had accomplished the work God gave Him to do.

We will follow the instructions for "redeeming the time" given in Ephesians: "Therefore be careful how you walk, not as unwise men, but as wise, making the most of your time, because the days are evil. So then do not be foolish, but understand what the will of the Lord is" (5:15-17). In these verses of Scripture I see three important steps in the time-management process:

GOALS   In order to make the most of our time we must "understand what the will of the Lord is" (v. 17) and make His goals our goals.

ANALYSIS   In order to make the most of our time (v. 16) we must take inventory: "Am I making the best use of my time now?"

PLANNING   In order to make the most of our time, we must "be careful how we walk" (v. 15)—looking ahead, planning our course.

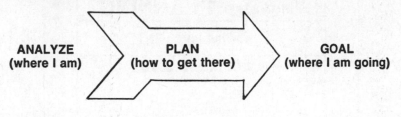

**ANALYZE**
**(where I am)**

**PLAN**
**(how to get there)**

**GOAL**
**(where I am going)**

**Figure 1**

I like to think of these three steps as the GAP method of time management: *Goals, Analysis, Planning*. It reminds me of the tremendous gap between my life and His. Ephesians 5 is an exhortation to close the gap. We are encouraged

to imitate Christ (5:1)

to walk in love, as Christ loved us (5:2)

to walk as His children (5:8)

to be filled with His Spirit (5:18)

to love our wives as Christ loved the church (5:25)

The three steps in Ephesians 5:15-17 are God's method for bridging the gap. They can be likened to three rungs up the ladder to total time management (figure 2).

# God's Method of Time Management
## *Ephesians 5*

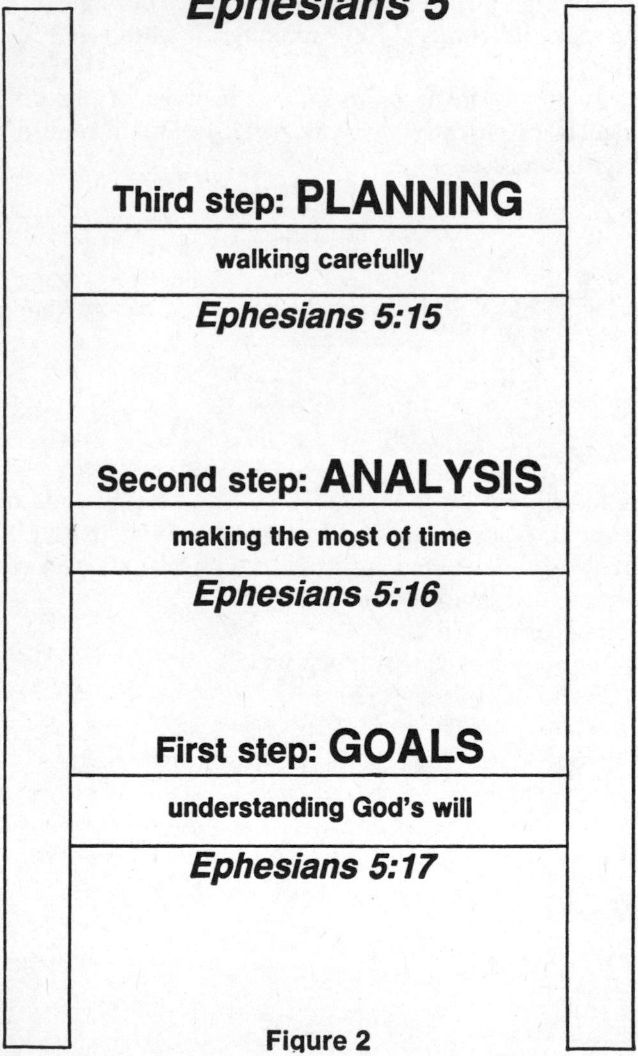

Third step: PLANNING

walking carefully

*Ephesians 5:15*

Second step: ANALYSIS

making the most of time

*Ephesians 5:16*

First step: GOALS

understanding God's will

*Ephesians 5:17*

Figure 2

# Section I
# GOALS

# 3

# Goals Motivate

The California coast was shrouded in fog that Fourth of July morning in 1952. Twenty-one miles to the west on Catalina Island a 34-year-old woman waded into the water and began swimming toward California, determined to be the first woman to do so. Her name was Florence Chadwick. She had already been the first woman to swim the English Channel in both directions.

The water was a numbing cold and the fog was so thick she could hardly see the escort boats. Millions were watching on national television. Several times, sharks had to be driven away with rifles to protect the lone figure in the water. Fatigue had never been her big problem in these swims—it was the bone-chilling cold of the water.

More than 15 hours later, numb with cold, she asked to be taken out. She couldn't go on. Her mother and her trainer, in the boat alongside, told her the shore was near. They urged her not to quit, but when she looked toward the California coast, all she could see was the dense fog, and she asked to be taken out.

Hours later, when her body began to thaw, she felt the shock of failure. She had been pulled out only a half-mile from the California coast.

A reporter asked, "What was it, Miss Chadwick, that kept you from swimming that last half mile?"

"It was the fog," she replied. "If I could have seen land, I could have made it. When you're out there swimming and you can't see your goal, you lose all sense of progress and you begin to give up." With no land in sight, her motivation was gone.

It was the only time Florence Chadwick ever quit. Two months later she swam that same channel and beat the men's record by two hours. She could see her goal (*Bits and Pieces*, Economics Press, July, 1979).

In most firms the marketing group comes up with a sales forecast for the year. Such goals help manufacturing and other departments plan ahead, but more important, they become targets to shoot for. If sales are behind, there is incentive to make up the difference by the next month. Each field salesman is given his quota to make. If these goals were not written down and distributed at the beginning of the year, I am convinced the sales level would remain constant or even decrease. The president of one firm said, "A sales forecast tends to be a self-fulfilling prophecy." Why? Because goals motivate.

The same is true for any field of endeavor—for a housewife organizing her household or a pastor praying for church growth. A list of goals becomes a personal scorecard to spur us on. We may not be competing against anyone but ourselves, but we want to do better than we have in the past. Having a tangible goal makes us put in that extra effort to reach it.

To motivate, the goal must be measurable; it must be formulated in such a way that we will know whether or not we have reached it. We should set a target date for completing it or it will be put off. It must also be realistic lest we become discouraged. A motivating goal is a future event which can be accomplished and measured in time and by performance.

When I give a time-management seminar to a church group, I sometimes get static: "You can't measure spiritual things. You're placing too much emphasis on performance. Our job is to obey God and leave the results to the Holy Spirit." What these Christians are saying is that *purpose* (a direction given by God) is OK, but a *measurable goal* is not.

## Jesus Had Goals

Even the Lord Jesus had measurable, God-given goals. How else would He have known that His hour had come and that He had accomplished the work His Father had given Him to do?

Consider the following: At 12 years of age, Jesus recognized that He must be about His Father's business (Luke 2:49); that's purpose and direction. Early in His ministry He spoke of "the works which the Father has given Me to accomplish" (John 5:36). The reason He could report that His mission was accomplished at the end of His life was that these works were measurable.

Jesus announced the goals of His earthly visitation at the beginning of His ministry. They were formulated before He came to earth and were recorded by the Prophet Isaiah 700 years before. After His baptism and temptation, Jesus returned to Nazareth (His hometown), entered the synagogue on the Sabbath and read the words of Isaiah: "The Spirit of the Lord is upon Me, because He anointed Me to preach the Gospel to the poor. He has sent Me to proclaim release to the captives, and recovery of sight to the blind, to set free those who are downtrodden, to proclaim the favorable year of the Lord" (Luke 4:18-19). Jesus closed the scroll and explained that He was the One commissioned to meet these five goals. All were accomplished by the end of His life.

## Paul Had Goals

Paul had goals too: "That I may know Him and the power of His resurrection, and may share His sufferings, becoming like Him in His death, that if possible I may attain the resurrection from the dead. Not that I have already obtained this or am already perfect; but I press on to make it my own, because Christ Jesus has made me His own. Brethren, I do not consider that I have made it my own; but one thing I do, forgetting what lies behind and straining forward to what lies ahead, I press on toward the *goal* for the prize of the upward call of God in Christ Jesus" (Phil. 3:10-14, RSV).

Then Paul speaks of what he had already attained (3:16). He viewed the Christian life as a race with many milestones along the way and a prize at the finish line. How would he have known he had attained anything unless his goals were measurable and realistic? At the end of his life he wrote, "The time of my departure has come. I have fought the good fight, I have finished the race, I have kept the faith. Henceforth there is laid up for me the crown of righteousness, which the Lord, the righteous judge, will award to me on that Day" (2 Tim. 4:6-8, RSV).

Why do you suppose Paul set goals? If we have no goals, that's exactly where we will end up—at no goal! Many Christians are strenuously running up and down the football field of life and never scoring, because they have no goals. How would you like to follow a leader who had no goals—who aimlessly drifted through life with no direction?

Imagine sitting in an airplane when the pilot comes on the speaker and says, "We have some good news and some bad news. First, the good news: We have plenty of fuel and we're making excellent time. Now the bad news: We're lost and we don't know where we're going!"

## God's Goals for Our Lives

I believe God has specific goals for every Christian. Some are general, like being conformed to the image of Christ. Others are more specific, like the development of our particular spiritual gifts or a call to a particular place of service. God does have a plan for our lives. "For I know the plans I have for you, says the Lord, plans for welfare and not for evil, to give you a future and a hope" (Jer. 29:11, RSV).

We have already seen how the time-management process outlined in Ephesians 5 requires that we "understand what the will of the Lord is" (v. 17, RSV); therefore, a crucial step in making the most of our time is to discern God's goals for our lives. "You have finished with the old man and all he did and have begun life as the new man, who is out to learn what he ought to be, according to the plan of God" (Col. 3:9-10, PH).

To pursue our own goals when they are at variance with God's goals is "foolish" (Eph. 5:17, RSV) and usually brings grief. Jonah had a measurable, realistic goal: to go to Tarshish, but it was contrary to God's goal: "Arise, go to Nineveh, that great city, and cry against it; for their wickedness has come up before Me" (Jonah 1:2, RSV). Tarshish was in the opposite direction from Nineveh. Nineveh was 530 miles to the east; Tarshish was 2,500 miles to the west on the tip of Spain. God called Jonah to be a street preacher in Nineveh. Jonah said, "Thanks, but no thanks; I'd rather take a leisurely Mediterranean cruise to sunny Spain." Jonah set sail, but the Lord didn't give up. He sent a storm; Jonah was thrown into the sea, swallowed by a whale, and regurgitated at the place where he began. "Then the word of the Lord came to Jonah the second time, saying, 'Arise, go to Nineveh, that great city, and proclaim to it the message that I tell you'" (Jonah 3:1-2, RSV). Jonah would have saved himself grief and time if he had followed God's goals instead of his own goals.

On the other hand, when God's goals become our goals, there's no limit to what we can accomplish. Paul said he was equal to every circumstance in the will of God, "I can do all things through Christ which strengtheneth me" (Phil. 4:13, KJV). Lack of ability or strength is not the problem; it is understanding what the will of the Lord is.

Satan's objective is to darken our understanding of God's will (Eph. 4:17-18). It is reassuring to know that God is more anxious for us to know His will than we are. The shepherd-sheep analogy in John 10 assures us that Jesus calls His own by name and leads us even when we are dumb and wayward.

I am convinced that the primary obstacle to knowing God's will is an unwillingness to do it—as in the case of Jonah. Our attitude is, "Lord show me Your will so I can see if it suits me." Jesus said the reason He knew God's will perfectly was because He did not seek His own will, but the will of God (John 5:30). If we are going to discover the will of God, we must: (1) make ourselves available as "living sacrifices," (2) resist conformity to the world's thinking, and (3) allow God to transform our thinking to conform with His will (Rom. 12:1-2). Through prayer we can successfully battle an unwilling disposition and have our minds renewed.

Don't get the idea that what you desire is always at variance with God's will. "Delight thyself also in the Lord; and He shall give thee the desires of thine heart" (Ps. 37:4, KJV). There is such a thing as the permissive will of God. Often, as we delight in the Lord, we come to the place where our desires have been transformed to correspond with His will. "God is at work in you, both to will and to work for His good pleasure" (Phil. 2:13, RSV). We will see later how God often gives us a desire that corresponds with our spiritual gift. I will do my best work for Christ when I am doing what I most enjoy.

How then can I discover God's goals for my life? The Scriptures outline four channels for guidance: the Word of God, the inward promptings of the Spirit, the ordering of circumstances, and counsel of godly Christians. Prayer is the key that unlocks each channel for guidance. I pray that God will bring Scripture to light revealing His will. I pray God will give peace about the right way. I pray He will open and shut doors to indicate His path. I pray He will confirm it through two or three witnesses (godly counsel). See Figure 3.

It is important to set sail toward some goal. It's very difficult to steer a ship dead in the water. We can flip the rudder back and forth with no response. It's better to be headed for the wrong goal than standing still. Then at least God can turn us around. Seneca, the Roman philosopher, said, "When a man does not know what harbor he is heading for, no wind is the right one."

Paul was heading for Asia to preach the Gospel when he was forbidden by the Holy Spirit to speak the Word there. He turned toward Bithynia and the Spirit did not permit it. Finally, he had a vision directing him to go to Macedonia (Acts 16:6-10). If Paul had not been obedient to God's previous leading (to preach the Gospel to the Gentiles), the Spirit may not have directed him further. Why should God give us more light if we're not walking by the light we have? Over 90 percent of God's will for our lives is found in the Bible. If we act on that, God will supply the missing instructions.

## Unachievable Goals

Some Christians avoid goal-setting because their pasts are strewn with unmet goals. They're discouraged by failure. If you're in this situation, it's safe to assume your goals were not realistic. On the

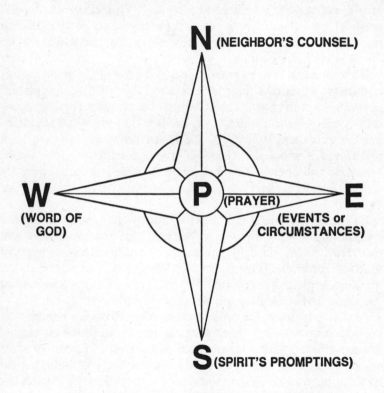

## THE COMPASS OF GOD'S GUIDANCE

### Figure 3

other hand, if you're reaching all of them, you need more challenge. Goals motivate because they challenge us to excel. There is the feeling of achievement and accomplishment when we reach them.

I like to think of a goal as a target. The bull's eye is 100. Concentric rings are 80, 60, 40, and 20. I aim for 100, but sometimes I hit 80 or even 20. But if I don't aim for 100, I will hit zero every time. Someone said, "I would rather attempt to do something great for God and fail, than to do nothing and succeed."

After Eisenhower won the Republican nomination for President from Robert Taft in 1952, a reporter asked Taft about his goals. He said, "My great goal was to become President of the United States in 1953." The reporter smirked, "Well, you didn't make it, did you?" He said, "No, but I became senator from Ohio!" (*Bits and Pieces*, Jan. 1980) He didn't hit 100, but 80, 40, or 20, depending on what you think of senators.

Even the Apostle Paul didn't always reach his goals. In his Second Epistle to the Corinthians, he explains why he had to abort his plan to visit them. In his Epistle to the Romans he speaks of his goal to preach the Gospel in Spain, but he probably never reached there because of his imprisonment. However, in striving for these goals he accomplished a great deal.

Charles Hummel of Inter-Varsity Christian Fellowship told me his training as a chemical engineer at M.I.T. ideally suited him for Christian work among college students. One might have supposed that Bible school and seminary would have been better preparation. "Not so!" said Hummel. God gave him the goal of a chemical engineering career to motivate him to get the maximum out of that training. He then redirected him toward another goal. Had Hummel missed God's will; had he taken a detour? I think not.

## Classifying Goals

Where do I begin? Do I write down any goal that pops into my head? What if I miss something important? A good way to approach goal-setting is to classify goals with respect to time and sphere of operation.

For example, a distinction should be made between long-range, yearly, monthly, weekly, and daily goals. I recommend getting alone with God for at least 24 hours to pray about long-range goals. We need to ask ourselves and God the following questions:

- When I appear at the Judgment Seat of Christ, what will be my major accomplishment in life?
- What do I want it to be?
- What does God want it to be?
- What is my spiritual gift and how will it contribute to my major accomplishment?
- Does my spiritual gift dictate a more realistic goal which will still be a major accomplishment?
- Which of my current activities will contribute most to my major accomplishment?
- What are the major obstacles to my reaching this goal?
- What should I be doing now to insure that I reach the goal?
- What should I be doing daily, weekly, monthly, and yearly to reach that goal?
- What other goals tend to pre-empt my major long-term goal or get in the way? What can I do to put them in their place?

Let's suppose your major long-range goal is evangelism; you want to be at the point where you are winning souls to Christ every week, and you're not there yet. You need a plan for getting there. A supportive *goal for the year* might be to attend a conference or seminar on evangelism sometime in the next 12 months. *Monthly goals* may include reading the biography of one great evangelist and one book on soul-winning. A *weekly goal* might be to memorize three verses that help communicate the Gospel. Or to be involved in your church's visitation program—sharing the Gospel weekly. *Daily goals* which support the ultimate goal would certainly include spending time alone with God in His Word and in prayer. Perhaps you could start a notebook of biblical principles for evangelism which you discover in your quiet times, and pray daily for individuals who are without Christ. At some point in the future you may want to set a goal of witnessing to at least one person each day, as Dawson Trotman of The Navigators did. If you don't have daily, weekly, and monthly goals you'll never reach your long-range goal.

Take a moment to set down a long-range goal. Then specify the yearly, monthly, weekly, and daily goals that will help you get there. Writing down goals is important; unwritten ones remain vague.

It is also good to set goals for each *sphere of your life*. I like the framework suggested in Luke 2:52: "Jesus increased in wisdom and in stature, and in favor with God and man" (RSV).

There are few worthwhile goals in life that don't fit into one of these spheres:

- To increase in wisdom (intellectual)
- To increase in stature (physical)
- To increase in favor with God (spiritual)
- To increase in favor with man (social)

If we follow Jesus, we can't afford to neglect any of the four.

My tendency is to neglect the physical. I pay too little attention to diet and physical condition. A number of years ago I read a book that reported that a high percentage of businessmen in my position develop heart disease. The book scared me, and I've been running ever since. I've been jogging for 12 years. I'm not sure I've learned to enjoy it, but I like the results. When I jog regularly, I feel better, am more alert mentally, have more energy, require less sleep, and have fewer colds. The net effect is that jogging is a great time-saver. In fact, if I jog 20 minutes daily, I require an average of 30 minutes less sleep a night.

Recently, I joined a racquetball club to make exercise even more enjoyable. I also hope to use it to support discipling and evangelism activities. If you find it difficult to pursue a goal, try combining it with something you enjoy.

The other three spheres are equally important. Young mothers, in particular, often feel the need for intellectual stimulus. A reading program or course at a community college may meet that need. To keep on top spiritually, a daily quiet time is a must. To "increase in favor with God" we should be serving Him as well—"trying to learn what is pleasing to the Lord" (Eph. 5:10). Social growth implies more than being friendly and going to parties. We are to "increase in favor" with people. This means looking for ways to serve and help others. It means doing a good job at work; it means pleasing my spouse, a parent, or a friend.

## Goals in Each Sphere of Life

Stop your reading now and jot down a few personal goals in the four spheres suggested in Luke 2:52.

Intellectual (increasing in wisdom)_____

*keep at least at 3.5 GPA average*

Physical (increasing in stature)_____

*run/exercise 4-5 times a week*
*at least 40 minutes*

Spiritual (increasing in favor with God)_____

*memorize Scripture*
*devote myself to prayer*

Social (increasing in favor with people) *get together*
*w/ Beth Koo.*
*be a servant*
*listen w/ my heart + not*
*just my ears.*

Use the *goals worksheet no. 1* (Exhibit 3-1) and classify your goals

**EXHIBIT 3-1 GOALS WORKSHEET NO. 1 (For you to fill in)**

| | LONG-RANGE | YEARLY | MONTHLY | WEEKLY | DAILY |
|---|---|---|---|---|---|
| INTELLECTUAL | | | | | |
| PHYSICAL | | | | | |
| SPIRITUAL | | | | | |
| SOCIAL | | | | | |

according to sphere and to time. If you don't attach a time frame to a goal, you will seldom get around to even starting it. Exhibit 3-2 is the same worksheet filled in with examples related to the overall goal of evangelism.

## Are They Measurable?

Writing these goals is the first step toward making them definite and measurable. "Don't be vague, but firmly grasp what you know to be the will of God" (Eph. 5:17, PH).

We must also think about the time frame. To be measurable, a goal must include the date of completion and a schedule for meeting that date.

A third step in making a goal measurable is to make sure the goal is formulated concretely. There should be no doubt as to whether the goal has been reached. For example, "to memorize Scripture" is *not* a measurable goal; to memorize a specific number of verses is.

In one of my time-management seminars, someone pointed out that not many goals in Scripture are measurable. For example, the Scriptures encourage us to hide the Word in our hearts (John 15:7), but never command us "to memorize a certain number of verses per week." This is because there is diversity within the body of Christ. You may have greater facility for memorization than I do. On the other hand, I may have greater facility next year than I do this year. The Scriptures allow for various levels of maturity and aptitude. As a result, the commands of Scripture are seldom specific and often hard to measure. It is the Spirit of God who applies them to individuals in different ways. We need to pray for the wisdom of the Spirit in formulating our goals.

## Are They Realistic?

Sometimes we become discouraged with goals because we're overly ambitious, and then we fail. We may try to take on the attributes of God. One pastor said, "Last year my goal was to be omnipresent; this year I decided to be more realistic and settle for omnipotence!"

Often we try to follow in the footsteps of a spiritual giant and

**EXHIBIT 3-2  GOALS WORKSHEET NO. 1 (Examples related to evangelism)**

| | LONG-RANGE | YEARLY | MONTHLY | WEEKLY | DAILY |
|---|---|---|---|---|---|
| **INTELLECTUAL** | Become proficient at apologetics. Able to answer any objection to the Gospel. | Attend one course or workshop on apologetics. | Read one book on apologetics. | Develop apologetic answer to one question through study. | Start and maintain a daily notebook on objections to the Gospel and their answers. |
| **PHYSICAL** | Maintain good physical condition with weight at 160 pounds. | Lose 20 pounds. Increase jogging to 2 miles daily. | Lose 4 pounds on average, until I reach 160 pounds. | Lose one pound. Play racquet-ball twice. | Avoid between-meal snacks. Jog one mile. |
| **SPIRITUAL** | Winning souls to Lord on a regular basis (one each week on the average). | Read through whole NIV Bible. Attend one seminar on evangelism. | Read one book on evangelism and/or a biography of a great evangelist. | Memorize 3 verses that share Gospel. Share with one person. | Maintain quiet time (one hour). Read 2-3 chapters in Bible. Pray for one person's salvation. |
| **SOCIAL** | Developing solid friendships with three non-Christians at any given time. | Developing friendship with one non-Christian with regular (monthly) activities together. | Invite one non-Christian into home for dinner. | Participate in church's visitation program. Introduce self to 5 new people. | Initiate conversation with one non-Christian. |

become discouraged when we find our capabilities overtaxed. The Word of God warns against this specifically: "Each man should examine his own conduct for himself. Then he can measure his achievement by comparing himself with himself, and not with anyone else" (Gal. 6:4, NEB). In other words, don't set a goal of memorizing 100 verses every week like Dawson Trotman if you haven't memorized any before. On the other hand, settling for one verse a month is not very challenging for most of us. We probably won't remember to memorize one. The idea is to compare how we're doing today with how we did last year to see if there's been growth.

Overly ambitious goals frustrate. In fact, Dr. Freudenberger says that the major causes of burnout are unrealistic goals and expectations (*Burnout: The High Cost of High Achievement*, Doubleday, p. 13). If you are in a leadership position, this is extremely important to remember. To inspire confidence, leaders must convince their people that their goals are achievable.

What if the only way out involves an unbelievable goal? I don't even have the faith to pray for it! A neat trick for converting an unrealistic goal to a realistic one is to break it down into several faith-sized subgoals. Nehemiah was faced with a formidable task—rebuilding the wall of Jerusalem. How did he go about it? By dividing the overwhelming task into many achievable parts. Each man was given responsibility for one small section of the wall (Neh. 3). Joshua was given the impossible task of conquering Canaan with all of its fortified cities and military superiority. He did it, not by attacking them all together, but by picking off one city at a time. Divide and conquer.

When John Baker was a high school junior, he surprised everyone by winning his first cross-country race, defeating the state champion, and setting a new record in the process. He focused on the runner in front of him, and set as his goal passing that runner. When he did, he set a new goal of passing the next runner, and then the next. He shut out of his consciousness the overall goal of winning the race. He concentrated on a realistic, achievable subgoal.

Suppose you are a salesman and your boss wants you to open

100 new accounts this year. Impossible? Before you give up, break the goal down into subgoals. One hundred new accounts for the year is only 2 a week, or 8 or 9 new accounts per month.

We sometimes refer to subgoals as *doable (do-able) activities*. The idea is to think backwards from the major goal and ask, "What activities or steps can be taken now to achieve that goal?" For the long-range goal of becoming an evangelist, doable activities include memorizing verses, praying daily for unsaved friends, starting a notebook of biblical principles for evangelism, sharing the Gospel weekly, reading books on soul-winning, and beginning to seek out training sessions on evangelism.

If you are having trouble getting started on your goal, identify an easy first step that will enable you to start. The chapter on *procrastination* will help you to eliminate other roadblocks.

Now take some of your more important goals on *goals worksheet no. 1* and transfer them to *goals worksheet no. 2* (Exhibit 3-3). *Goals worksheet no. 2* forces you to make sure your goals are measurable by asking such questions as, "How will I know it happened?" and "When do I want it to happen?" Identifying a first step toward the goal will also help keep it realistic and believable. Setting faith-sized subgoals and milestones along the way establishes a route and makes the goal reachable. Refer to the examples given in Exhibit 3-4 to help you fill in yours.

To summarize, the key ingredients of good goal-setting are:

- Make sure your goals are God's goals. Spend time in the Word and in prayer. Be willing to conform to God's plan for your life.
- Write your goals. Be specific. If it's not in writing, it's not a goal. An unwritten desire is only a pipedream that will probably never happen. If it's in writing, it's a commitment.
- Make sure your goals are measurable in time and performance. Be concrete. Schedule completion. If the goal is vague, you can never be certain when you've arrived. There's no satisfaction in the accomplishment when goals are fuzzy.
- Be sure your goals are realistic. If you don't believe that with God's help you can achieve it, you won't pay the price for it. Break the unreachable goal into subgoals.

**EXHIBIT 3-3   GOALS WORKSHEET NO. 2 (For you to fill in)**

| | SPECIFIC GOAL (What do I want to happen?) | MEASUREMENT (How will I know it happened?) | WHEN? | HOW? SUBGOALS (A first step toward this goal would be:) |
|---|---|---|---|---|
| INTELLECTUAL | | | | |
| PHYSICAL | | | | |
| SPIRITUAL | | | | |
| SOCIAL | | | | |

**EXHIBIT 3-4 GOALS WORKSHEET NO. 2 (Examples related to evangelism)**

| | SPECIFIC GOAL (What do I want to happen?) | MEASUREMENT (How will I know it happened?) | WHEN? | HOW? SUBGOALS (A first step toward this goal would be:) |
|---|---|---|---|---|
| INTELLECTUAL | Proficient at Christian apologetics. | Able to answer any intellectual objection to the Gospel. | Within one year. | Start reading one book on apologetics (e.g., Paul Little's *Know Why You Believe*). Start keeping notebook on objections to the Gospel and their answers. |
| PHYSICAL | Maintain good physical condition. | Lose 20 pounds, weigh 160 pounds. Jogging 2 miles daily. | In 20 weeks. | Start sport of racquetball. Avoid between-meal snacks. Jog at least one mile each day. |
| SPIRITUAL | Lead persons to the Lord regularly. | Leading an average of one person to Christ each week. | Within 2 years. | Pray for one person's salvation each day. Start memorizing verses which share Gospel. Start looking for opportunities to share 4 spiritual laws. |
| SOCIAL | Develop friendships with non-Christians on a regular basis. | Regular activities with at least one non-Christian each month. | 6 months. | Start to go out of way to befriend non-Christians. Participate in church's visitation program. Introduce self to one new person today. |

## Should Goals Be Shared?

In my time-management seminars, I sometimes suggest that people take goals home and share them with their spouse or with a close friend. This works well provided you pick one who is not overly skeptical or negative: "I remember the last time you tried to lose 20 pounds—it took you a year to take them off and one month to put them back on!" That kind of response does not motivate. It turns a realistic goal into an impossible one. Nehemiah kept his mission to rebuild the wall to himself until he had surveyed the ruins and made all the arrangements (Neh. 2:11-16). If your spouse is negative, keep your goal a secret and let the results be a surprise. Just to think of hearing "What happened to you?" or "Have you lost weight?" is motivating.

Benefits may result from sharing goals, however.

• It may strengthen your commitment and resolve. Sharing a goal with others as well as with God is like a twofold cord that is harder to break. You will be ashamed to give up.

• Family members and friends can sometimes help you achieve your goals if they know what they are. My wife answered the phone because I needed uninterrupted time to write this book. Colleagues at work are more apt to leave us alone if they know we're working on a project. A friend may loan me a book on racquetball if he has heard I'm taking up the sport.

• Sharing goals reduces the chance of misunderstanding. One family told me how disappointed they were with their vacation. Dad thought he was going fishing. He could almost smell the fish frying over the campfire. Mom thought they were going to the lake to give her a break from household chores. How nice it would be to lie in bed, knowing there was no breakfast to prepare! Junior saved his money for weeks to learn to water-ski. Dad never did understand why Mom wasn't thrilled about sleeping in a tent or why Junior wasn't excited about the small motor on the rowboat they rented.

• Relationships are strengthened through sharing common goals. We are naturally attracted to people who have similar goals; we tend to withdraw from people whose goals are different. We often find our friends among those with whom we work, whether at the office or at church. People working together are bent on accomplishing a common goal. A sense of common destiny links us together.

After formulating goals, share them with some who have the gift of encouragement. Invite them to share their goals too. You may find you are closer to each other as a result.

# 4

# Priorities: Ours or His?

In our training classes, Christians are taught to pray for elders and others in church leadership. Without warning, one young lady approached me and asked, "What's your biggest problem?" Caught off guard, I snapped back, "Establishing priorities!" The more I think about it, my reflex answer was right. There is always more to do than I have time for.

The telephone is always ringing with people who want counseling. Every invitation to preach is an exciting opportunity. New committees, like black holes, are constantly sucking me in. Job problems can easily take 80 instead of 40 hours. How nice it would be to take off for the beach with the family—not to mention the myriads of fascinating hobbies I never have time to pursue.

Whenever I feel pressed for time, I have the same unnerving dream. I'm surrounded on all sides by enormous piles of magazines and books. Stacks loom over my head, grow larger by the moment, and then fall over on me. Then the awful realization stabs me—I'm never going to have enough time to read all these magazines and books.

What should my priorities be? A fit-looking gentleman told me my body was not in good shape. He explained that I could not possibly expect to do all I was doing with a weak body, that physical fitness should be a top priority, and I should join the athletic club. I agreed.

After I had preached a sermon, someone else told me I should become more conversant in world affairs. After all, if a preacher is to be relevant, he must understand the society in which we live. She said, "I suggest you take a course in political science. Keeping yourself informed is a top priority!" She was right!

A man told me he had been reading *Daws* and was impressed with his 40-day prayer vigil. He said, "We need more prayer here; prayer should be a top priority." I agreed. Then he reminded me of Martin Luther's prayer priority. The application was obvious: How can someone attempt to do as much as I'm doing without more prayer?

Priorities! I should be working out, studying political science, and spending more time in prayer, but the day is only so long. I had a brilliant idea! I got an exercise bicycle and mounted a music stand on the handle bars to hold a book. I discovered I could pedal with one eye open for reading and one eye closed for praying. Marvelous!

It seemed like the perfect solution until someone came along and said, "It's your family we're worried about. You're spending so much time doing family counseling, we wonder if you're neglecting your own. Your family is your top priority!" So there was only one thing to do: Get three more exercise bicycles so we could ride together with books on the handlebars, and with each of us having one eye open and one closed.

About that time someone came along and said, "I don't think you're getting enough rest. You're going to burn out!"

Who's right? They're all right. As we've seen, Jesus increased in all four spheres (Luke 2:52)! If I neglect any, it is to my detriment. If I don't keep physically fit, mentally alert, spiritually in tune, and socially alive, my ministry and work will suffer. But how do I balance priorities?

The Bible is the best book on priorities. If God gives goals, He certainly gives priorities. We've seen His priority already: "But seek first His kingdom and His righteousness, and all these things shall be yours as well" (Matt. 6:33, RSV). "All these things" refers to other priorities mentioned in the chapter. If we are serious about making His priorities our priorities, it's important to know what our priorities are now and whether they conflict.

## Existing Priorities

Everyone operates under some kind of priority system. We may not have a list, but we can pinpoint them in Matthew 6 by asking three questions:
- What am I anxious about?
- How do I spend my time?
- What do I buy with my money?

In this passage we see that Jesus cautioned His disciples against anxiety (6:25-34). We only worry about things which are important to us. If we are anxious about something, it probably ranks high among our existing priorities.

Jesus also cautioned against spending time accumulating wealth and material possessions (6:19-24). If we spend lots of time on sports or watching TV, it says something about our priorities. How we spend our time is a clue.

Jesus spoke of the Gentiles buying the best food, drink, and clothing (6:31-32). How we spend our money shows our priorities and our goals.

As one man put it: "I spend eight hours earning money, another eight hours spending twice what I earn, and most of the remaining eight hours wondering why I can't sleep."

Jesus is not saying "these things" are unimportant; "Your heavenly Father knows that you need them all. But seek first His kingdom and His righteousness" (Matt. 6:32-33 RSV).

## What's Our Number-one Priority?

Even if all the goals you listed on your worksheet were realistic, there may be too many of them. Ask God which goals are most important to Him. None of us wants to arrive at the Judgment Seat of Christ only to find we discarded the goal that was most important to Him. As Peter Drucker says, "We not only want to do things right, we want to do the right things."

We can discover God's priorities for our lives through prayer and the Word of God. In this chapter we want to develop a priority grid from the Scriptures by which we can test our goals. A good place to begin is with the great commandment.

A lawyer came to Jesus and asked Him a question, "Teacher, which is the great commandment in the Law?" (Matt. 22:36) Jesus' answer provides a framework on which we can hang all our priorities. He said, " 'You shall love the Lord your God with all your heart, and with all your soul, and with all your mind.' This is the great and foremost commandment. And a second is like it, 'You shall love your neighbor as yourself.' On these two commandments depend the whole Law and the Prophets" (Matt. 22:37-40).

Jesus' priorities are clear:
- God is more important than people.
- People are more important than things. (Things don't last for eternity, but God and people do.)

The Greek word for love in this passage is *agapao*—an unselfish love, ready to serve. Jesus says we must love God with all our faculties: intellect, emotions, and volition. Also we are to love others as we naturally love ourselves.

Not only did Jesus preach these priorities, He lived them. Even as a 12-year-old boy He said, "I must be about My Father's business" (Luke 2:49, KJV). Again and again, time with His Father took priority over time with people.

Even though He was God, the second Person of the Trinity, He felt the need to spend much time alone with the Father in prayer. After a grueling day healing the sick in Capernaum, He got up early and "departed into a solitary place, and there prayed" (Mark 1:35, KJV). Before selecting the 12 Apostles, "He went out into the hills to pray; and all night He continued in prayer to God. And when it was day, He called His disciples, and chose from them 12, whom He named apostles" (Luke 6:12-13, RSV). After the feeding of the 5,000, perceiving that the multitudes were about to come and take Him by force to make Him king, Jesus withdrew again to the hills to pray (Mark 6:46; John 6:15).

Jesus had to say *no* more than once in order to say *yes* to His Father. Surely if there was enough time in three-and-a-half years for Him to complete what God gave Him to do, there is enough time in our lives too. We must say *no* too. If we are too busy to get time alone with God each day, we are too busy! It is time to say *no*.

The apostles learned this lesson well. They were so busy distributing food, they neglected higher priorities. They asked the congregation to appoint seven men to be in charge of this service in order that they might devote themselves to prayer and the ministry of the Word (Acts 6:1-4).

Of course, we may love the Lord just as much through service as in devotion, but He puts a premium on devotion. The story of Mary and Martha in Luke 10 illustrates this priority. When Jesus arrived at the home of the sisters, Mary immediately sat at Jesus' feet to listen. Meanwhile Martha was busy preparing the meal. Martha, who was left to do all the work herself complained, "Lord, do you not care that my sister has left me to do all the serving alone? Then tell her to help me"(v. 40). The Lord answered, "Martha, Martha, you are worried and bothered about so many things; but only a few things are necessary, really only one, for Mary has chosen the good part" (vv. 41-42). In our Lord's eyes, time spent with Him has a greater priority than service—even when it's done for Him.

In our eyes, Mary was a lazy bum. Martha is to be commended for her hard work; she wanted everything just right for the Master. Perhaps Martha was a workaholic like most of us. A simpler meal would have allowed her time to listen to the Master as well. Martha's problem is our problem. We are "worried and bothered about so many things" we neglect what is most important. God wants *us*—not what we do!

A widower who was trying to be both father and mother to his 12-year-old girl felt he never had enough time with her, and he was looking forward to the Christmas vacation. He was disappointed when his daughter spent all but mealtimes in her room. Finally on Christmas morning, she presented her father with his Christmas present—a pair of hand-knit socks. "Daddy," she said, "I was so afraid I wouldn't get them done in time! I've been working on them in my room! Do you like them?" "Darling," he replied, gathering her up in a big hug so she couldn't see his tears, "Of course I do; they're beautiful! Thank you very much."

In his heart, he was saying, "I can buy socks anywhere; I really wanted your time, your attention, and your love. I wanted to talk to you and do things with you." Good intentions, but wrong priorities!

On the other hand, we are never to use our devotion to God as an excuse to avoid meeting the needs of our fellowman. In the same chapter as the account of Mary and Martha (Luke 10) we read the story Jesus told about the man attacked by robbers and left in the ditch for dead. A priest and a Levite, seeing the man, passed by on the other side, for if he was dead and they touched him they would be ceremonially unclean for seven days. The priest would not be able to perform his religious duties in the temple. In not stopping, these men thought they were following higher priorities, but Jesus commended a despised Samaritan who stopped, and finding the man alive, gave aid and made arrangements to care for him at an inn. Jesus used the example of the Samaritan to demonstrate what it means to "love your neighbor as yourself." The story of the Good Samaritan and the incident at the home of Martha follow immediately after Jesus taught the two great commandments (Luke 10:27). The two together delineate priorities in loving God and our neighbors.

Putting God first results in an even higher sense of responsibility to others. Obedience to God means loving others. Jesus put His Father's business ahead of His earthly parents to reach the theologians in the temple. He neglected the multitudes to spend time in prayer for a more effective ministry to the same multitudes. The apostles delegated the distribution of food to seven deacons to free themselves to teach the Word of God. Mary was better motivated to serve others, having spent time at the Master's feet. The good Samaritan's love for God overcame his prejudice to help a half-dead Jew.

There are also times when love for our neighbors is a prerequisite for loving God. For example, Jesus said, "If you are offering your gift at the altar, and there remember that your brother has something against you, leave your gift there before the altar and go; first be reconciled to your brother, and then come and offer your gift" (Matt. 5:23-24, RSV). It is interesting that we often do not remember a sin against a neighbor until we come to God. Coming to God first is still the key! If God seems distant, we need to ask why, make it right, and then come again.

The same priorities apply in matters of authority. God has ordained the powers that be; we are to obey the governing authorities (Rom. 13:1-7). Nevertheless, there is sometimes a conflict between the authority of those over us and the authority of God. Peter and the apostles were clear about their priorities. "We must obey God rather than men" (Acts 5:29). The same priorities apply in any authority structure—whether employer-employee, husband-wife, or parent-child. To obey God is our priority. In so doing, we are better able to serve our fellowman.

Two years ago, I went through a crisis in priorities at my job. An interim president asked me to do something which violated my conscience before God. I explained my convictions, but he continued to press me. If I refused to comply, I ran the risk of being fired and jeopardizing my career goals. Of course, there is really no choice in a case like this: "I must obey God rather than men." I stood my ground and was fired. A new president was installed a month later, and I was reinstated! God says, "those who honor Me, I will honor" (1 Sam. 2:30, RSV). He must be first.

## People Priorities

Granted that God must always have priority over people, some of our biggest problems of priority are with people. In Galatians we read "Let us do good to all men, and especially to those who are of the household of faith" (6:10). Since Paul was the apostle to the Gentiles and spent much of his time evangelizing the lost, one wonders if he followed these priorities. Remember, however, that no matter where he was, Paul always went first to the synagogue (the "household of faith"). Even on his missionary journeys, Paul gave prime time to follow up new converts. He spent more than two years strengthening the church at Ephesus.

Jesus directed His preaching primarily at Israel. He instructed His disciples, "Go nowhere among the Gentiles, and enter no town of the Samaritans, but go rather to the lost sheep of the house of Israel. And if any one will not receive you or listen to your words, shake off the dust from your feet as you leave" (Matt. 10:5-6, 14, RSV). Jesus did not spend a lot of time cajoling folk who were not interested in what he had to say. He spent prime time building His disciples and virtually no time with those who rejected His message.

So now the priority grid becomes:

- God
- Believers
- Nonbelievers

"Doing good" for fellow believers is in itself a witness to an unbelieving world. "By this all men will know that you are My disciples, if you have love for one another" (John 13:35).

## Priorities within the Household of Faith

There is often a misunderstanding of priorities within the home and the church. There is no question that our devotion to Christ takes precedence over the family. Jesus said, "Anyone who wants to be My follower must love Me far more than he does his own father, mother, wife, children, brothers, or sisters—yes, more than his own life, otherwise he cannot be My disciple" (Luke 14:26, LB). Yet we all have known ministers who burned out for Christ and let their kids go down the tubes. Usually, the neglect of our families is not because we loved God more, but because we loved others more. The question, then, is how do we assign priorities of time and ministry within the body of Christ?

Pat King in her book *How to Have All the Time You Need Every Day* relates how she was involved in a ministry to inner-city kids. After a planning session for a theatrical production aimed at keeping the kids off the streets that summer, Pat dashed home at noon to see how her kids were doing. As she arrived at the house, a police car pulled up behind her. Sitting in the backseat were her eight- and nine-year-old sons—frightened to death. While she was gone, the two boys had stolen some matches from her kitchen and gone to a vacant lot to light firecrackers (a no-no). The lot had caught fire and the boys were apprehended by the neighbors. It suddenly became obvious to Pat which kids she should be trying to keep off the streets that summer. She called the inner-city office and resigned (Tyndale, p. 60).

Surely my immediate family is that part of the family of God for which I have greatest responsibility. Paul says failure in that responsibility disqualifies a man for leadership in the local church. "An overseer . . . must be one who manages his own household well, keeping his children under control with all dignity (but if a man does not know how to manage his own household, how will he take care of the church of God?)" (1 Tim. 3:2, 4-5) In Titus we read that the children of an elder must be believers (1:6). If a man can't lead his own children to Christ, how will he lead anybody else?

I know of one minister whose family had turned away from him, because his income was not enough to support their needs. He was counseled to take a leave of absence from his church and get a job for a couple of years. His family interpreted this to mean that he really did care about them—even more than the church. He's back in a flourishing ministry now with his family 100 percent behind him. "If any one does not provide for his own, and especially for those of his household, he has denied the faith, and is worse than an unbeliever" (1 Tim. 5:8).

The story of Eli shows the tragic results of a priest who neglected his duty as a father. The Lord rebuked Eli for not restraining his sons Hophni and Phinehas who were also priests (1 Sam. 3:13); He accused Eli of honoring his sons above the Lord (1 Sam. 2:29). God chastened Eli by taking the lives of his two sons and Eli's life too (1 Sam. 2:31-34; 4:17-18). Apparently Eli did a good job of training Samuel who was entrusted to his care, but he failed in disciplining his own sons. Never was a priest so severely punished for neglecting his family. If we fail with our families, success with a Samuel means little.

These principles should give some consolation to young mothers who feel trapped and unfulfilled. The daily regimen of dirty diapers, toilet training, broken washing machines, and one-word conversations with a two-year-old is like a prison. "My ministry will go down the tube!" lamented one mother. Little did she realize her ministry was just beginning. New priorities, but the Lord's!

The imprisonment of the Apostle Paul in Rome sent shock waves around the Christian world. It was obviously a ploy of Satan to silence the evangelist. Yet Paul could write from his prison cell, chained to a Roman soldier, "Now I want you to know, brethren, that my circumstances have turned out for the greater progress of the Gospel, so that my imprisonment in the cause of Christ has become well-known throughout the whole praetorian guard" (Phil. 1:12-13). Paul's priorities had not changed, but circumstances had.

Like Paul, a young mother needs to see her kids to whom she is chained as a ministry, to say *no* to competing priorities outside the home. She need not feel guilty about saying *no* to the women's missionary society while she is tending her own mission field. However, she needs to take care not to let her greater priorities suffer—time with the Lord and time with her husband.

For the young mother, the daily devotional time often becomes inconsistent or even nonexistent. There are constant interruptions; she is always getting up to feed the baby, and she never gets enough sleep. On top of her exhaustion, there is sometimes post-partum depression and a general hormone imbalance. She misses church a lot because the kids are frequently sick. Her personal time with the Lord needs top priority if she is to grow spiritually. "Women shall be preserved through the bearing of children [i.e., the childbearing years] if they continue in faith and love and sanctity with self-restraint" (1 Tim. 2:15). Indeed, continuing in these is the key to surviving any trial.

To preserve the daily quiet time during the childbearing years requires strong self-discipline and some ingenuity. I know of two women who trade off baby-sitting to allow each other uninterrupted time with God. Susanna Wesley, the mother of John Wesley and 18 other children, taught them not to disturb her when she had an apron over her head. A portable prayer closet!

My wife was "preserved" through the childbearing years by a godly woman 10 years older who encouraged her in the faith and prayed with her—sometimes over the din of wailing kids.

Paul says older women should encourage the young women to love their husbands and love their children in that order (Titus 2:4). Statistics indicate that a marriage is most vulnerable to divorce at two times: after the first child or after the kids leave the nest. The first child is so demanding, a wife may neglect her husband. He may then seek female companionship elsewhere. After the kids leave the nest, husband and wife have time for each other, but wonder if they have anything in common. The young mother should never forget she has been called by God to be a wife first and a parent second. He doesn't demand polished floors or clean cupboards; He does insist that you love your husband and your children.

Pat King (*How to Have*, pp. 40-42) tells of a friend, Irene, who was in much demand as a Bible teacher. Her husband, Mike, was a nominal Christian who went to church but took no part. Irene's priority list looked like this:

- God
- Teaching women's Bible studies
- Family

One day the Lord spoke to her through Ephesians 5:22 (AMP) "Wives be subject—be submissive and adapt yourselves—to your own husbands as [a service] to the Lord." Did she really love Mike? Did she put him first? She was everything to the Christian community she served, but not everything to Mike.

Irene dropped her outside activities and began to spend more time with Mike. When the church asked her to teach, she declined. When a friend asked her to lead a home Bible study, she refused. She stayed home with Mike; she watched TV with him, jogged with him, played cribbage, and made love to him. Irene dropped out of the picture as far as a visible Christian ministry was concerned. It was painful.

The subsequent two years were like "walking in a dark valley." Mike continued as a so-so Christian. Then in the middle of the third year, something stirred in Mike. He began to lead devotions and to do some teaching. His commitment to Christ solidified and he began to develop into a Christian leader. Irene realized that if she had remained in the limelight, Mike would have been too threatened to venture out. Today, at Mike's insistence, they together teach a class for couples. They have new priorities:

- God
- Each other
- Other Christians

The Mosaic Law places the highest priority on the husband-wife relationship. "When a man takes a new wife, he shall not go out with the army, nor be charged with any duty; he shall be free at home one year and shall give happiness to his wife whom he has taken" (Deut. 24:5). This meant that even a priest, when newly married, was relieved of his priestly duties for one year to nurture his marriage and lay the foundation for a successful home. A man's ministry must begin at home and overflow into the larger family of God. If he fails at home, his ministry among the people of God will be frustrated. If he neglects his wife, even his prayer life will be hindered (1 Peter 3:7 ).

## A Biblical Priority Grid

Now we can set down a biblical priority grid with which to test our goals:
 I.  God (Matt. 22:36-38)
 II. People (Matt. 22:39-40)
    A. Immediate family (1 Tim. 5:8)
       1. Spouse (Eph. 5:21-22, 25)
       2. Children (Eph. 6:4)
    B. Family of God (John 13:35)
    C. Non-Christians (Gal. 6:10)

Take your list of goals developed in the last chapter and scrutinize them with respect to this grid. Ask yourself three questions:
*Are my personal development goals selfish?* Notice that the priority grid is others-directed. Someone has said that Jesus' whole life could be summarized in the word "others." Goals to develop your intellectual abilities or to build a strong body are legitimate provided they will better equip you to minister to others. God gave gifts and talents to men "for the equipping of the saints, for the work of service, to the building up of the body of Christ" (Eph. 4:12). Psychologists agree that we will never be satisfied achieving goals focused exclusively on ourselves. To be totally satisfying and motivating, our goals must contribute to or meet the needs of others. Even unregenerate man affirms it is more blessed to give than to receive.

*Are my goals too materialistic?* The priority grid says nothing about "things." "Things" will pass away; God and people go on living for eternity! There's nothing wrong with having income goals or investment goals if they will meet the needs of your immediate family or the body of Christ. In other words, "Everything created by God is good, and nothing is to be rejected, if it is received with thanksgiving; for then it is consecrated by the Word of God and prayer" (1 Tim. 4:4-5, RSV).

At age 18, Robert Laidlaw decided to start giving one-tenth of his income to the Lord. At age 20, he wrote in his diary, "Before money gets a grip on my heart, by the grace of God I enter into the following pledge with my Lord that:

I will give *10 percent* of all I earn up to_____.
If the Lord blesses me with_____,
I will give *15 percent* of all I earn.
If the Lord blesses me with_____,
I will give *20 percent* of all I earn.
If the Lord blesses me with_____,
I will give *25 percent* of all I earn.
The Lord help me to keep this promise for the sake of
Christ who gave all for me."

At age 25 he wrote, "I have decided to change the graduated scale and start now giving half (50 percent) of all my earnings." God so prospered Robert Laidlaw that he became one of the most successful businessmen in all New Zealand. At age 70 he wrote, "I want to bear testimony that, in spiritual communion and in material things, God has blessed me one hundredfold, and has graciously entrusted to me a stewardship far beyond my expectations when, as a lad of 18, I started to give God a definite portion of my wages" (Tom Rees, *Money Talks*, Hildenborough Hall, pp. 28-29). Who would suggest that Robert Laidlaw's goals were unspiritual or materialistic?

*Are some of my goals really "subgoals"?* If some of your goals seem too mundane, think of them as *subgoals* or *support goals* for a major goal. For example, mowing the lawn or fixing the dryer may seem like inconsequential goals, but they may be part of an integral maintenance program which insures your spouse's well-being and shows her you love her. Likewise, getting a raise may help meet needs of family members. Going to a party may make you want to go off and read Ecclesiastes, but it could also broaden your social contacts and open doors for evangelism.

After scrutinizing your list, fill in the *priorities worksheet* (Exhibit 4-1). A sample worksheet has been filled in for your reference (Exhibit 4-2). Notice that a single goal may appear in several blocks. For example, the goal of reading the Bible through in a year will:

- Draw me closer to God.
- Help me in soul-communication with my wife.
- Assist me in bringing up my children in the fear of the Lord.
- Give me a better understanding of Scripture for evangelizing.

## Prioritizing Goals

The *priorities worksheet* is a first step toward getting a feel for what your major goals should be. The final step is to come up with a list of all your goals in order of priority. As a start, try grouping your goals under three headings:

- A – Top Priority
- B – Very Important
- C – Important

Don't forget to pray for the Lord's mind.

If you're having difficulty prioritizing, ask yourself:

- Assuming I can reach all of these goals before I die, which will I be remembered for?
- What would I like to do when I retire?
- Am I happy in my present job or occupation?
- If I knew the Lord were coming back one year from today, which goals would I like to accomplish before then?
- For which of these goals am I willing to spend one hour each week?

Take your top three goals, write them on an index card, and tape them to your mirror where you will see them each morning. Then share them with your spouse or a close friend.

**EXHIBIT 4-1  PRIORITIES WORKSHEET (For you to fill in)**

|  | INTELLECTUAL | PHYSICAL | SPIRITUAL | SOCIAL |
|---|---|---|---|---|
| 1. GOD |  |  |  |  |
| 2. SPOUSE |  |  |  |  |
| 3. CHILDREN |  |  |  |  |
| 4. FAMILY OF GOD |  |  |  |  |
| 5. OTHERS |  |  |  |  |

**EXHIBIT 4-2  PRIORITIES WORKSHEET (Example)**

| | INTELLECTUAL | PHYSICAL | SPIRITUAL | SOCIAL |
|---|---|---|---|---|
| **1. GOD** | Read 2 to 3 chapters in Bible each day. Read theological commentary on same. | Lose 20 pounds. (My body is the temple of the Holy Spirit. 1 Cor. 6:19). | Increase prayer time to one hour daily; maintain prayer diary — recording prayer requests and answers. | Spend 30 min. daily in intercessory prayer. Maintain list of others' needs to bear burdens. |
| **2. SPOUSE** | Read one book together with wife every two months and discuss weekly. | Lose 20 pounds to please my wife. | Pray daily with wife. Have one good session each week to share what God has been teaching us as individuals. | Take wife to lunch once a week. |
| **3. CHILDREN** | Be available to help with homework. Arrange bimonthly educational experience (museum, exhibition, forum, etc.). | Jog or play racquetball with sons each week. | Pray daily with sons. Use meal times to teach spiritual truths and to discuss as a family. | Spend weekly time with sons individually. Plan a family outing each month. |
| **4. FAMILY OF GOD** | Teach Sunday School class on Christian apologetics. | Play racquetball with someone I'm discipling each month. | Spend 5 hours weekly preparing for Sunday School class. Carry on one-on-one discipling each week. | Attend small-group fellowship weekly. Have one group of Christians in for dinner each month. |
| **5. OTHERS** | Be able to answer any intellectual objection to the Gospel. | Play racquetball with one non-Christian at least once a month. | Share *Four Laws* with one non-Christian each week. | Have one non-Christian or family into home for dinner each month. |

# 5

# Getting in on God's Plan

In 1887, a 60-year-old man paid for his groceries with a $20 bill. The clerk happened to notice that the green ink was coming off on her hands. But she knew it couldn't be counterfeit; she had known Immanuel Linger for years. He was an upstanding citizen. She gave him his change and went on with her work, but the incident bothered her. Finally, she called the police.

Two officers came to the grocery store and looked at the bill. One said, "Nothing wrong with that! I wish I had 100 of them!" The other responded, "If it's genuine, how is it the ink is coming off?" So the officers got a warrant and searched through Linger's house. Up in the attic, they found what they were looking for: an artist's easel with brushes and paint. On the easel was a $20 bill near completion. Immanuel Linger counterfeited $20 bills by painting them. He was so skillful that if the clerk's hands had not been wet, Linger might never have been discovered.

After Immanuel Linger went to jail, three of his paintings brought $16,000 at an auction. The irony is that it took the artist approximately the same length of time to paint a $20 bill as it did to paint a portrait worth over $5,000. Immanuel Linger was a talented man, but his talents were wasted and perverted.

The day is coming when God will judge the secrets of men and the waste of our talents will be revealed (Rom. 2:16). The abuse, misapplication, and neglect of talent will bring shame. Some of us, like the unprofitable servant in the Parable of the Talents, have buried our talents in the earth where they lie dormant and unused. God intends for us to use the talents and spiritual gifts He gives. God's plan for our lives revolves around our spiritual gifts. They should be the focus of our ministries. If we are unaware of our gifts, if our goals and priorities don't include their development; we will be the losers (1 Cor.3:15) at the Judgment Seat of Christ.

We have noted that the first step in the time-management process is to "understand what the will of the Lord is" (Eph. 5:17). If we want to avoid spinning our wheels, we must set our goals and priorities "understanding what the will of the Lord is." "The new man [who] is out to learn what he ought to be, according to the plan of God" (Col. 3:10, PH).

An essential for getting in on God's plan is to know what our spiritual gifts are and how to develop them. We do this by setting goals and priorities which develop our gifts for God's glory. Nothing can burn us out faster than trying to pursue ministries for which we are not spiritually endowed.

"But I don't have a spiritual gift!" you complain. God says you do! "As each one has received a special gift, employ it in serving one another" (1 Peter 4:10). "But to each one is given the manifestation of the Spirit for the common good" (1 Cor. 12:7). If God says we have gifts, we have them.

"Well, how come I don't know it?" you ask. Did you know what your natural talents were when you were born into the world? Just as you received a natural talent at the time of your natural birth, you receive at least one spiritual gift at the time of your spiritual birth. Often it takes years before a natural talent is disclosed and begins to manifest itself. Likewise, I know of no Christian who knew what his spiritual gift was at the time he became a Christian. Talents and gifts are discovered with time and use as we grow physically and spiritually.

When Prince Charles was born into the royal family, he had no idea of the vast resources at his disposal. He may still be discovering them. Likewise, spiritual gifts are not discovered overnight. But why is it that a gift can lie hidden and dormant for a lifetime?

I believe it is Satan's strategy to keep us in the dark concerning our spiritual gifts so we will never use them. At the very least, he intends to confuse us and sidetrack us in their development. The obstacles are familiar ones.

## Obstacles to Discovering Our Gifts

Four major passages in the New Testament deal with spiritual gifts (Rom. 12:1-8; 1 Cor. 12; Eph. 4:7-13; and 1 Peter 4:10-11). In Romans 12, Paul gives us four obstacles which prevent the discovery and development of a spiritual gift: selfishness, pride, envy, and laziness. Just as God seldom reveals His will to someone who is unwilling to obey, we will remain in the fog concerning our spiritual gifts until we root these attitudes out of our lives. God abhors the abuse of gifts as much as their neglect.

*Selfishness.* I have been in prayer meetings where people have been seeking spiritual gifts purely for self-gratification. In James we read the reason our prayers remain unanswered is because we ask with the wrong motives (James 4:3).

The Apostle Paul appeals to us to present our bodies for spiritual service; "I beseech you therefore, brethren, by the mercies of God, that ye present your bodies a living sacrifice, holy, acceptable unto God, which is your reasonable service" (Rom. 12:1, KJV). The word *sacrifice* is the very antithesis of selfishness. Our bodies are to become living sacrifices—including all our members, faculties, and natural talents. A prerequisite for developing the spiritual gifts mentioned is to make ourselves available. "Lord, take all of me and use me in Your service." Talents and faculties used for ourselves will never develop spiritual gifts.

In Romans 12:1 we see how natural talents dovetail with spiritual gifts. Let's suppose you have a natural talent for speaking. If you go out and speak for your own glory, your ministry will be devoid of supernatural power. On the other hand, if you've given the Lord your talent for His service, God may use it as a channel for some spiritual gift. A facility for speaking could be used as a channel for the gifts of prophecy, teaching, and exhorting. A musical talent could be used as a channel for these three as well, particularly the gift of exhortation (stimulating the faith and works of others). I always wondered why born leaders can do well in business and still be a flop in the church. I'm convinced it's because they haven't been willing to dedicate that talent to the Lord.

On the other hand, making your body a "living sacrifice" may mean the Lord will ask you to sacrifice a talent to make room for a spiritual gift. C.T. Studd, founder of the Worldwide Evangelism Crusade, was greatly used of God on several continents. When he came to Christ, Studd was a talented cricketer. The press referred to him as a "born cricketer." He continued to play after committing his life to Jesus Christ and received honors like no other cricketer before him.

One day, Studd realized that cricket had become an idol to him. It was more than recreation; he was obsessed with it. It had become more important than serving his Lord. He wrote, "The question came to me: 'What good will it do anybody in the next world for me to have been the *best* cricket player that has ever been?'" He dedicated his life afresh to Jesus Christ and never played cricket again. He went to the mission field instead, because winning souls was more important than winning cricket matches. (N. P. Grubb, *C. T. Studd, Cricketer and Pioneer*, Religious Tract Society, p. 57). Studd, by his sacrifice, proved that the plan of God for his life was perfect. "And be not conformed to this world: but be ye transformed by the renewing of your mind, that ye may prove what is that good, and acceptable, and perfect will of God" (Rom. 12:2, KJV).

## Serve One Another

A servant's heart (the opposite of selfishness) is essential in the development of spiritual gifts. "As each one has received a special gift, employ it in *serving* one another, as good stewards of the manifold grace of God" (1 Peter 4:10). The man who wants to lead just to get others to serve him will never develop the gift of leadership. The ministry of gifts is always others-directed rather than self-directed. God gave gifts to men "for the equipping of the saints for the work of *service*, to the building up of the body of Christ" (Eph. 4:12).

*Pride.* Nothing quenches a spiritual gift faster than pride. Churches have split because some thought they had a monopoly on spiritual gifts. They looked with disdain on others who didn't have the gifts they had. Paul warned against such thinking: "I say to every man among you not to think more highly of himself than he ought to think; but to think so as to have sound judgment, as God has allotted to each a measure of faith. For just as we have many members in one body and all the members do not have the same function, so we, who are many, are one body in Christ, and individually members one of another" (Rom. 12:3-5).

One of the pitfalls of pride is the delusion that God has called us to do it all. As a result, we burn ourselves out on hundreds of activities for which we are ill-equipped. I have known men who were so busy trying to practice *all* the gifts that they never discovered their own. We need to recognize our limitations, learn to say a gracious *no* and encourage others more gifted than ourselves to fill the gap. Paul pleads for a sane estimate of our abilities in accordance with faith (Rom. 12:3).

A second problem with pride is that it focuses attention on a person and detracts from God's glory. Spiritual gifts are divided into two broad categories: speaking gifts and serving gifts (1 Peter 4:11). "Whoever speaks, let him speak, as it were, the utterances of God; whoever serves, let him do so as by the strength which God supplies; so that in all things God may be glorified through Jesus Christ, to whom belongs the glory and dominion forever and ever. Amen" In other words, if we have a speaking gift, we are not to speak our words, but God's Word. Speaking gifts are for the glory of God—not to get people enamored with our ideas or intellect. If you have a serving gift, don't do it in your strength, but in God's. Serving gifts are exercised to give God the glory— not to bring credit to ourselves. If our motives are to bring glory to ourselves, why would God even want to show us our gifts?

*Envy* is the third obstacle to developing a gift. Often we are so envious of other people's gifts that we become blind to our own.

A 38-year-old scrub woman would go to the movies and sigh, "If only I had her looks." She would listen to a singer and moan, "If only I had her voice." Then one day someone gave her a copy of the book *The Magic of Believing*. She stopped comparing herself with actresses and singers. She stopped crying about what she *didn't have* and started concentrating on what she *did have*. She took inventory of herself and remembered that back in high school she had a reputation for being the funniest girl around. She began to turn her liabilities into assets. A few years ago Phyllis Diller made over $1 million in one year. She wasn't good-looking and she had a scratchy voice, but she could make people laugh.

The Apostle Paul urges us to evaluate our gifts with sound judgment "as God has allotted to each a measure of faith" (Rom. 12:3). An underestimate of one's gift can be as bad as an overestimate. He refers to the analogy of the human body, which he develops more thoroughly in 1 Corinthians 12, and shows that each Christian has a role to play in the body of Christ. Don't let the fact that you're not a hand keep you from being what you were intended to be—a foot. A lame foot slows down the whole body. There is a sense in which every believer is indispensible to the body of Christ. There is a sense in which all other believers are dependent on you. Don't look at other believers and say, "Oh, if I were as gifted as she is," because there is a sense in which no one else can do what God gifted you to do.

*Laziness.* Developing a spiritual gift can be hard work. Paul wrote to Timothy, "Do not neglect the spiritual gift within you. . . . Take pains with these things; be absorbed in them, so that your progress may be evident to all. Pay close attention to yourself and to your teaching; persevere in these things" (1 Tim. 4:14-15).

One of Ripley's "Believe It or Not" items pictured a plain bar of iron worth $5. The same bar of iron if made into horse shoes would be worth $50. If it were made into needles, it would be worth $5,000. If it were made into balance springs for fine Swiss watches, it would be worth $500,000. The raw material is not as important as how it's developed. God says we have spiritual gifts, but their worth to Him will be dependent on how we develop them.

For example, you may have the gift of teaching, but you will never be able to teach the Word of God effectively until you become familiar with the whole counsel of God. To be an effective Bible teacher is a lifelong process. God may have given you the gift of teaching at the very beginning of your Christian life, but it was like a diamond in the rough. It needed polishing and faceting. The tragedy is that many Christians leave that diamond in the mud.

## A Basic List of Gifts

In our key passage, Paul urges the Christians at Rome to exercise seven gifts: prophecy, serving, teaching, exhorting, giving, leading, and showing mercy (Rom. 12:6-8). Peter spoke of two general categories: speaking and serving gifts (1 Peter 4:11). The seven gifts of Romans 12 break down as follows:

|  |  |
|---|---|
| SPEAKING GIFTS | Prophesying<br>Teaching<br>Exhorting |
| SERVING GIFTS | Serving<br>Giving<br>Leading<br>Showing mercy |

A more extensive list of gifts is given in 1 Corinthians 12, but I believe that they are all derived from the basic list of seven listed in Romans 12. Further, the Word of God commands every believer to practice in varying degrees all seven of these gifts:

PROPHESYING (speaking to others for God)
"Pursue love, yet desire earnestly spiritual gifts but especially that you may prophesy" (1 Cor. 14:1).

SERVING (meeting the needs of others)
"Through love *serve* one another" (Gal. 5:13).

TEACHING (helping others understand and apply God's truth)

"Let the Word of Christ richly dwell within you, with all wisdom *teaching* and admonishing one another" (Col. 3:16).

EXHORTING — (stimulating the faith and works of others) "But *exhort* one another daily" (Heb. 3:13, KJV).

GIVING — (sharing yourself and your goods to meet the needs of others) "*Contributing* to the needs of the saints" (Rom. 12:13).

LEADING — (coordinating the activities of others to achieve common goals) "He must be one who *manages* his own household well, keeping his children under control with all dignity" (1 Tim. 3:4).

SHOWING MERCY — (comforting and empathizing with others) "Put on a heart of *compassion*, kindness, humility, gentleness and patience, bearing with one another and forgiving each other" (Col. 3:12-13).

We discover our gifts by *practicing* all the gifts and exploring them. We will soon find that God has given a special enabling for at least one or more.

Paul wrote that we should judge our gifts "each according to the degree of faith apportioned by God" (Rom. 12:3, AMP). I take this to mean that as I practice the seven gifts listed in Romans 12, the one I exercise with greatest faith is my special spiritual gift.

## Discovering Spiritual Gifts
Let's look at each gift. Which could you exercise with the greatest faith and liberty?

*Prophecy.* Most people think of prophecy as foretelling the future. Many of the prophets of the Old and New Testaments did foretell the future, but their primary call was to "forth-tell" the Word of God. In this capacity they confronted individuals and nations with their sins. They sometimes unveiled the future, but more often unveiled the sinful hearts of men. Therefore, prophecy is speaking forth God's message under the power and conviction of the Holy Spirit. Somebody said the difference between a preacher and a prophet is that a preacher has to say something, but a prophet has something to say. The Apostle Peter had the gift of prophecy. He was fearless in confronting members of the Sanhedrin with their sin of rejecting Christ. When Ananias was deceptive about selling a piece of land, Peter asked, "Ananias, why has Satan filled your heart to lie to the Holy Spirit? . . . How is it that you have contrived this deed in your heart? You have not lied to men but to God" (Acts 5:3-4, RSV). Peter spoke for God who struck Ananias dead.

Sometimes, prophets are misunderstood. Their frankness and directness may be viewed as harsh—particularly by those with the gift of mercy. Their demand for righteous living may be interpreted by some as legalistic. Their strong desire to speak for God makes them poor listeners. This may be the prophet's greatest shortcoming—jumping to conclusions about sin and being unwilling to listen. Yet we need to thank God for those with the gift of prophecy. They are God's spokesmen in our midst. Their word (God's Word) has changed our lives.

*Serving.* I once met a man who had equipped his pickup truck with several extra cans of gasoline, water, a tow chain, and long jumper cables. I thought he was being overly cautious and kidded him about living by the boy scout motto "Be Prepared." He explained that he took a special delight in helping stranded motorists. He also had a plentiful supply of tracts in that sanctified pickup truck. The man had a gift of serving.

A servant is someone who would rather do good than look good. Ka Tong Gaw (of Taylor University) tells of his first day in Bible school. Having come from a well-to-do home, he was accustomed to having servants at his disposal. Upon arrival at Bible school, he found the washroom in the dormitory so dirty he reported it to the headmaster. Almost immediately there were steps down the hall and when he looked out, he was shocked to see the headmaster with bucket and rags. A few minutes later the headmaster knocked on Ka Tong's door to report the washroom was clean. He not only had the gift of leading, he had the gift of serving.

Paul commended Timothy for his gift of serving. "I have no one else of kindred spirit who will genuinely be concerned for your welfare, for they all seek after their own interests, not those of Christ Jesus. But you know of his proven worth that he served with me in the furtherance of the Gospel like a child serving his father" (Phil. 2:20-22).

Even "Timothys" may be misunderstood. They may be so eager to serve others that they neglect their families. Or they may be so obsessed with meeting practical needs that some may accuse them of disinterest in the spiritual.

If you have the gift of serving, your biggest problem is your inability to say *no*. You can easily wear out serving others. You are always taking on more responsibility than you can handle. This leads to inner tensions. Even Timothy had stomach problems.

I thank God for those with the gift of serving. They seem to always be there when we need them. Several months ago, the timing chain went out on our van. It wasn't worth paying what the garage would charge to fix it. To further complicate matters, I had a conference to go to and several speaking engagements. But a brother who has the gift of serving said, "Mark, let me fix it for you." The exercise of his gift freed me to exercise mine.

*Teaching.* When Luke describes Apollos, he gives us an excellent definition of a teacher. "He was an eloquent man, well-versed in the Scriptures. He had been instructed in the way of the Lord; and being fervent in Spirit, he spoke and taught accurately the things concerning Jesus. . . . He greatly helped those who through grace had believed, for he powerfully refuted the Jews in public, showing by the Scriptures that the Christ was Jesus" (Acts 18:24-28, RSV).

Those with the gift of teaching have a real knack for explaining.

They present truth systematically. They generally have an insatiable hunger for God's Word.

We have all benefited from the clear exposition of Scripture by those with the gift of teaching. But teachers can be misunderstood too. Preoccupation with studies is often interpreted as disinterest in people. Sometimes, they retreat into their world of books, shutting out everyone around them—even their own families. This is often the teacher's biggest problem, becoming such a bookworm he has no time for people. There is also the danger of becoming puffed up with knowledge.

*Exhorting.* We usually think of exhorting as *admonishing,* but the word is also used for *encouraging.* The Greek word is *parakaleo* and is used to describe the Holy Spirit—the "Comforter." It refers to someone who comes alongside of another to help. My definition of exhorting (which seems to fit all the biblical references) is "stimulating the faith and works of others."

One who has the gift of exhortation is generally an able counselor. If you are getting more and more people coming to you for help, it may be a note from the Holy Spirit saying, "This is your gift."

The Apostle Paul had the gift of exhortation; his epistles are filled with it. He writes the job description for the use of his gift in Colossians, "And we proclaim Him, *admonishing* every man and teaching every man with all wisdom, that we may present every man complete in Christ. And for this purpose also I labor, striving according to His power, which mightily works within me" (1:28-29).

Exhorters are sometimes thought of as meddlers. They are deeply concerned about the spiritual condition of others. They will go out of their way to reprove and restore a brother or sister who has sinned. They take an active role in bearing burdens. They sometimes offend in this process, but "faithful are the wounds of a friend" (Prov. 27:6, RSV).

*Giving.* If you think the wealthy have a monopoly on this gift, you are mistaken. Jesus pointed to the example of the poor widow who put two mites into the temple treasury, "Truly I say to you, this poor widow put in more than all of them; for they all out of their surplus put into the offering; but she out of her poverty put in all that she had to live on" (Luke 21:3-4). Obviously, in God's eyes, real giving doesn't depend on the size of our bank accounts. You can be a millionaire and give 90 percent of your profits to the Lord or you can be a poor widow and give 2 pennies. Both can have the gift of giving. It is simply sharing ourselves and our goods to meet the needs of others.

Even givers can be misunderstood. When the widow gives her last $20, we think she's foolish. Some teenagers have trouble understanding why they must sacrifice so their father can give to a needy missionary family overseas.

The primary danger faced by those with the gift of giving is vulnerability. They are often sucked in by unscrupulous people who take advantage of their generosity. They are sometimes impulsive and subjective in their giving.

Thank God for those with this gift. Could any serve the Lord fulltime without the support of givers?

*Leading* (Administration). Perhaps the best test to see if you have this gift is to find out whether anybody is following you. General Eisenhower used to demonstrate leadership with a simple piece of string. He would put it on the table and say, "Pull it and it will follow you wherever you wish. Push it and it will go nowhere at all." You pull when you motivate by your example. President Harry Truman said it is the only way to "get others to do what they don't want to do and make them like doing it."

Nehemiah stepped into a demoralized and discouraged city to motivate and mobilize hundreds to rebuild the Wall of Jerusalem. He accomplished that incredible task in 52 days. He did it by inspiring confidence in God, but he also had the ability to plan and organize the activities of others to achieve their common goal.

Even Nehemiah was misunderstood. He was accused of being power-hungry—of being on an ego trip (Neh. 6:6-7). Leaders are sometimes accused of being more interested in a project than in the workers, and this probably is their most vulnerable point.

The common denominator in all growing works of God is leadership. What makes one church prosper while another in the same area stagnates? Leadership. I have worked with Christian businessmen's committees and Christian women's clubs in Massachusetts, California, Colorado, Utah, Oregon, and Texas. Some are growing; others are floundering. What makes the difference? Leadership.

*Showing Mercy.* This is the supernatural ability to sense when people are hurting in order to comfort and commiserate with them. The person who shows mercy can weep with those who weep and rejoice with those who rejoice (Rom. 12:15). He is adept at bearing another's burdens (Gal. 6:2), and is more faithful in intercessory prayer.

The one with the gift of mercy shows mercy "with cheerfulness" (Rom. 12:8). This is the sort of person who can be cheerful about any call for help—even at 2 A.M. This is the sort of person who can forget his own problems long enough to cheer up another who is down. "A happy heart is a good medicine and a cheerful mind works healing, but a broken spirit dries the bones" (Prov. 17:22, AMP).

Barnabas, whose name means "son of encouragement," pleaded with the Apostle Paul to give John Mark a second chance after his desertion and failure. This is typical of those with the gift of mercy. Whereas the prophet writes him off, the merciful maintain hope even in a failure. For this reason, it is often a person with the gift of mercy who is instrumental in restoring a backslidden Christian.

Prophets often misunderstand the merciful—thinking they are not firm enough. To them the merciful seem too weak—too diplomatic. Because they are sensitive about the hurts of others, they appear to be taking up another's offense.

The greatest danger for the merciful is in bearing so many burdens that he becomes depressed. Perhaps the admonition to show mercy with cheerfulness is designed to counteract this.

Bill Gothard (Institute in Basic Youth Conflicts) compares the seven gifts of the Spirit by showing how each gift might respond to an accident at dinner. The hostess drops the dessert on the floor.

The *server* says, "Here, let me clean it up."

The *leader* says, "Jim, would you go get the mop? Sue, if you will help clean up, Mary and I will fix another dessert."

The *giver* says, "I'll go out and buy another dessert."

The *merciful* says, "Don't feel badly, it could have happened to anyone."

The *prophet* says, "That's what happens when you're not careful."

The *teacher* says, "Clearly, the reason it fell is that it was unbalanced; the tray was too heavy on one side."

The *exhorter* says, "To avoid this in the future, you should use both hands."

There is a beautiful balance in the diversity of these seven gifts. When there is strife and misunderstanding in the church, almost always it can be traced to a failure to appreciate the function of other gifts in the body.

Perhaps now you have a better feel for what your primary gift might be. Here's a check list of seven questions to help you in your thinking:

• What kind of ministry do you enjoy most?

The root word for gift is *charisma* which comes from the word "char" meaning joy. There will be joy and personal fulfillment when you develop and exercise your spiritual gift.

• Which of your ministries is most fruitful?

Which ministry does God bless the most? Do you see conviction of sin when you preach? Do you see people get excited about biblical truth when you teach? Do you see people take action when you exhort? Do people follow your leadership and support you? Do people frequently come to you for counsel?

• Which builds up the body of Christ the most?

That's why gifts are given: "for the equipping of the saints for the work of service, to the building up of the body of Christ" (Eph. 4:12).

• Which glorifies God the most?

Remember 1 Peter 4:10-11, "As each one has received a special gift, employ it ... so that in all things God may be glorified through Jesus Christ, to whom belongs the glory."

• What spiritual abilities do others see in you?

Do others express more appreciation for your efforts in one ministry than in another?

• Which ministry are you asked to do again and again?

There is a demand within the church for Spirit empowered ministry. When people see it, they can't get enough of it.

• Are there ministries you've tried, but never been asked to repeat?

You may think you're gifted at some ministry, but if others don't think so, they won't benefit. For example, you may long to develop a counseling ministry based on a suspected gift of mercy, but if no one comes for help, you had better look elsewhere. If you think you know what your gift is, share it with your spouse or a close friend. Do they agree? Confirmation from others, including your pastor or those in church leadership, is important.

## Developing Spiritual Gifts

Once you have a fix on your gift, it must be developed. You are to put your heart and soul into ministries which develop your gift.

I like the way J. B. Phillips paraphrases Romans 12:6-8: "Through the grace of God we have different gifts. If our gift is preaching, let us preach to the limit of our vision. If it is serving others let us concentrate on our service; if it is teaching let us give all we have to our teaching; and if our gift be the stimulating of the faith of others let us set ourselves to it. Let the man who is called to give, give freely; let the man who wields authority think of his responsibility; and let the man who feels sympathy for his fellows act cheerfully."

You cannot develop your gift apart from involvement in some ministry of the local church. Paul says gifts are given "for the work of service, to the building up of the body of Christ" (Eph. 4:12). Since every believer has a spiritual gift, it follows that every believer should be active in a ministry that builds up the body of Christ. But the national statistics show that less than 20 percent of born-again Christians are actively involved in their local church. Eighty percent of the people are letting 20 percent of the people do all the work. No wonder the people who are involved are getting tired and weary; they're carrying more of a load than God meant them to carry.

It's like a football game. Twenty-two men are down on the field over-exhausted and desperately in need of rest, and 22,000 are in the stands desperately in need of exercise. The greatest need in the local church is for the spectators to come down out of the stands on to the playing field to become functioning team members of the God Squad.

Find a ministry and exercise your gift. If you believe your gift is teaching, study the Word of God systematically and share it with others. If you think you have the gift of leadership (administration), find a church committee lacking direction and volunteer to lead it. If yours is the gift of mercy, begin to visit patients in hospitals and nursing homes. Remember, gifts are not medals to be displayed, but mops and buckets designed to serve. Unless you have a servant's heart and hands, you will never develop your gift.

## Goals and Priorities That Reflect Gifts

Look back over the goals you've set for yourself. You may want to alter your goals if you have only now become aware of your gift. It may be you have assumed goals and responsibilities God never intended you to have. If they have nothing to do with your gift, they need to be scrutinized and perhaps discarded.

The idea is to specialize in your gift. Paul didn't tell Timothy to become well-rounded in all of the gifts; he said, "Stir up the gift of God, which is in thee" (2 Tim. 1:6, KJV). This takes dedication, determination, and persistence; you can't do that with all seven. Notice again the idea of concentration in the Phillips' paraphrase of Romans 12:7, "If it is serving others, let us concentrate on our service; if it is teaching let us give all we have to our teaching." Strive for excellence. The Quaker theologian Elton Trueblood wrote, "It is an affront to our Maker to live on the level of mediocrity when we could exhibit excellence."

The general framework for goals and priorities discussed previously will remain. The biblical priority grid directs me in applying my gift as follows:
- God
- My own family
- The family of God
- Others

God comes first. If my gift is teaching, I may teach in other areas, but I have a responsibility to teach His truth and righteousness first. I must spend time with God daily for Him to teach me so I can teach others.

My family comes second. God would never give me the gift of teaching if He did not mean it to be applied to my own family. "Train up a child in the way he should go: and when he is old, he will not depart from it" (Prov. 22:6, KJV). "And these words, which I command thee this day, shall be in thine heart: And thou shalt teach them diligently unto thy children" (Deut. 6:7 KJV). I am to love my wife "as Christ also loved the church. . . having cleansed her by the washing of water with the Word" (Eph. 5:25-26).

The family of God, the church, the body of Christ comes third. I will not refuse invitations to teach (where humanly possible) because this is what God has called me to do. If I have fulfilled my responsibilities to my family, there may be times when I will have to say no (even to them) to permit me to exercise my gift. If I am to teach, I must prepare—alone with God. This means saying no to other opportunities for ministry. I need to do a little less in order to study a little more.

My fourth priority includes those outside of the fold of Christ. I will teach the way of salvation as I have opportunity. Further, I will attempt to "equip the saints for evangelism" through the teaching of the Word.

How about the personal goals? (based on Luke 2:52)
- Intellectual
- Physical
- Spiritual
- Social

I must use my *mind* to assimilate biblical truth and proclaim it. I must be prepared intellectually to make a defense to everyone who asks me to give account for my faith (1 Peter 3:15). This may mean spending time in other books besides the Bible, and perhaps taking courses to expand my mental capacity.

I must stay in shape *physically* or my effectiveness in study and teaching will diminish. Above all else, I must stay on top *spiritually* by maintaining my channels of communication with God. It is only when I have a clean heart and a right spirit that I can teach transgressors His ways and see sinners converted to God (Ps. 51:10-13).

A teacher has *social* responsibilities also. My audience will turn me off if I'm not one of them. I cannot closet myself in an ivory tower—coming out only to teach.

Now take the gift you believe God has given you and work it through the *priorities worksheet* (Exhibit 5-1). Concentrate on short-range goals to get you started. Then do a second sheet focusing on long-range goals. If you have a teaching ministry now, you may seek to expand long-range into a radio or writing ministry. If you're reaching one group of people now, think about others God may want to reach in the future. Do this prayerfully, recognizing God's sovereignty over the use of His gift. Make it your purpose to get in on *His plan* for the use of your gift.

**EXHIBIT 5-1  PRIORITIES FOR DEVELOPING MY SPIRITUAL GIFT**

|  | INTELLECTUAL | PHYSICAL | SPIRITUAL | SOCIAL |
|---|---|---|---|---|
| 1. GOD |  |  |  |  |
| 2. SPOUSE |  |  |  |  |
| 3. CHILDREN |  |  |  |  |
| 4. FAMILY OF GOD |  |  |  |  |
| 5. OTHERS |  |  |  |  |

# Section II
# ANALYSIS

# 6

# Be Wise—Analyze

During the War of 1812 ships of the British Royal Navy approached the harbor of St. Michaels, a fishing village on the eastern shore of Maryland. The British command believed that it had found a vulnerable target, and in its eagerness neglected to send a spy ashore. Meanwhile, the villagers, aware of their peril, had extinguished all lights in the village and hung every available lantern in the trees of the adjacent forest. All night the British troops lobbed cannonballs into the target—most of which fell among the trees.

What can we learn from this story?

- Identifying our target (or goal) may be more difficult than we think.
- Aiming at the wrong target (or goal) can be enormously costly in terms of energy, money, or other resources.
- Early analysis can identify wrong targets and redirect efforts toward right ones.

There is nothing Satan likes better than to see a Christian fritter away time and resources in pursuits that do nothing to advance the cause of God's kingdom. Satan, like the town of St. Michaels, is very successful at making wrong targets appear worthwhile. Sometimes, even though we know the right goals, we pursue the wrong ones.

Along with establishing goals, setting priorities, and understanding the will of the Lord, we need to analyze the use of our time (second rung on the ladder, Figure 2). In Ephesians we read, "Therefore be careful how you walk, not as unwise men, but as wise, making the most of the time, because the days are evil. So then do not be foolish, but understand what the will of the Lord is" (5:15-17).

The *King James Version* reads, "Redeeming the time, because the days are evil" (Eph. 5:16). The Greek word translated "redeem" means to buy back what is lost. The idea is to put to use time that we would otherwise waste. The concept of redeeming the time implies that time is precious and worth money.

A plumber was called to a hotel to get a cat out from between the ceiling and the floor where the plumbing was located. The hotel manager was flabbergasted to receive a bill for $25. He asked that the bill be itemized and received this reply: "Called 'Kitty-Kitty' 125 times at 20¢ a call."

How we spend our time is far more important than how we spend our money. Money mistakes can be corrected, but time is gone forever. Though we can't borrow a minute from either yesterday or tomorrow, we can "redeem the time" by eliminating *time-wasters* and instituting *time-savers*. To do this, we must know *how* we are spending our time. We can't "redeem" wasted time if we don't know where we're wasting it.

The psalmist was conscious of the need to analyze our use of time. "So teach us to number our days, that we may apply our hearts unto wisdom" (Ps. 90:12, KJV).

William Borden, while still a sophomore at Yale, wrote in his spiritual diary, "Yesterday I figured up where my times goes each week and found that about 35 hours are wasted somewhere. I'm going to see if I can't systematize so as to get the most use out of them" (Mrs. Howard Taylor, *Borden of Yale*, Moody Press, p. 90).

Notice that "making the most of your time" (Eph. 5:16) is linked with "understand what the will of the Lord is" (5:17). Our objective is to analyze *how* we are spending our time by comparing our goals (what we *want* to do) with our use of time (what we're actually *doing*).

## Taking a Time Inventory

A *time inventory* is an accounting of how we use our time. There are two types: the *total-time inventory* and the *time-sample inventory*. In the first, we keep track of everything we do for one or two weeks. In the other, the idea is to take samples of what we are doing at various times during the day. The trick is to take enough random samples to make the results statistically valid. It can be shown that taking 10 samples each day for 10 days will produce an error of no more than 10 percent with a confidence level of 95 percent. To make sure the samples are random, I use a telephone book (a handy table of random digits) to select the time intervals between samples (e.g., 57, 26, 74, 06, 66, 60, 53, 59, 39, 41). I then set a pocket timer or wrist alarm to go off after the next specified time interval. When the timer goes off, I write down what I'm doing at the time. If the buzzer went off while I was on the phone 10 different times during 10 days, it means I spend 10 percent of my time on the phone. A gadget that beeps at random intervals 30 times during the working day is available for slightly under $1,000. At every beep, you press a coded button which signifies what activity you are involved in at the time of the beep. At the end of the day it will read out your time inventory.

In this book we will use the *total-time inventory*. It is more accurate, less complicated, and less embarrassing. (If you're in a meeting, you don't have to explain why your pocket timer went off.) Most time-management books suggest a log sheet like the one shown on the next page (Type A) in Exhibit 6-1. The day is divided into 15-minute segments. Enter your various activities and add up the number of segments in each activity to get a total for the day.

Personally, I like to write down times as I go along (Type B in Exhibits 6-2 and 6-3). This way I get a precise accounting of five-minute phone calls and other interruptions. To do this you must glance at the clock and jot down the time when you finish one task and begin another. At first it's hard to remember to check the time when interrupted, but after a day or two, you'll get the hang of

## EXHIBIT 6-1   TOTAL-TIME INVENTORY (TYPE A)
### Wednesday, February 24

| | | | |
|---|---|---|---|
| 6:00 | Quiet time | 3:00 | R & D staff meeting |
| | | | |
| 6:30 | | 3:30 | |
| | Jog | | |
| 7:00 | Shave and shower | 4:00 | |
| | Dress | | Read technical journals |
| 7:30 | Breakfast & family pray. | 4:30 | |
| | Drive to work | | |
| 8:00 | Prepare monthly report | 5:00 | |
| | | | Plan for tomorrow |
| 8:30 | | 5:30 | Drive home |
| | | | Talk with wife |
| 9:00 | | 6:00 | Help Greg with homework |
| | | | |
| 9:30 | | 6:30 | Supper — family devotions |
| | | | |
| 10:00 | Prepare outline/seminar | 7:00 | Roughhouse with Tim |
| | | | Get set for Bible study |
| 10:30 | Gather slides/seminar | 7:30 | Neighborhood Bible study |
| | | | |
| 11:00 | | 8:00 | |
| | | | |
| 11:30 | Return phone calls | 8:30 | |
| | | | |
| 12:00 | Take wife out to lunch | 9:00 | Talk with Warner about |
| | | | decision for Christ |
| 12:30 | | 9:30 | |
| | | | |
| 1:00 | | 10:00 | Open mail |
| | | | |
| 1:30 | Review mail | 10:30 | Prepare sermon outline |
| | | | |
| 2:00 | | 11:00 | Go to bed |
| | Answer letters | | |
| 2:30 | | 11:30 | |
| | Review R & D reports | | |

**EXHIBIT 6-2** TOTAL-TIME INVENTORY AT WORK (TYPE B)
Thursday, February 25

| CLOCK TIME | ACTIVITY | TOTAL MINUTES |
|---|---|---|
| 8:00 - 8:25 A.M. | Phone calls to East Coast | 25 |
| 8:25 - 9:00 | Review patent situation | 35 |
| 9:00 - 9:20 | Compose letter on patents | 20 |
| 9:20 - 9:45 | Miscellaneous correspondence | 25 |
| 9:45 - 9:50 | Dave interrupts with question | 5 |
| 9:50 - 10:00 | Resume correspondence | 10 |
| 10:00 - 11:15 | UF review meeting | 75 |
| 11:15 - 11:35 | Finish correspondence | 20 |
| 11:35 - 11:55 | Read Bob's report | 20 |
| 11:55 - 12:05 P.M. | Comments to Bob | 10 |
| 12:05 - 12:25 | Lunch at desk; read *Wall Street Journal* | 20 |
| 12:25 - 12:40 | Prayer time (door shut) | 15 |
| 12:40 - 1:20 | Run errand to bank | 40 |
| 1:20 - 1:40 | Return two phone calls | 20 |
| 1:40 - 2:30 | Boss drops in to review progress | 40 |
| 2:30 - 2:40 | Return one phone call | 10 |
| 2:40 - 3:30 | Begin to write article for journal | 50 |
| 3:30 - 3:40 | Troubleshooting call | 10 |
| 3:40 - 4:20 | Resume writing paper | 40 |
| 4:20 - 4:30 | Answer secretary's question | 10 |
| 4:30 - 5:00 | Resume writing paper | 30 |

**EXHIBIT 6-3**  TOTAL-TIME INVENTORY OUTSIDE WORK (TYPE B)
Thursday, February 25

| CLOCK TIME | ACTIVITY | TOTAL MINUTES |
|---|---|---|
| 6:00 - 6:45 A.M. | Quiet time | 45 |
| 6:45 - 7:00 | Jog | 15 |
| 7:00 - 7:15 | Shave and shower | 15 |
| 7:15 - 7:30 | Dress | 15 |
| 7:30 - 7:40 | Breakfast | 10 |
| 7:40 - 7:45 | Family prayer time | 5 |
| | | |
| 5:15 - 5:30 P.M. | Talk to wife — change clothes | 15 |
| 5:30 - 6:15 | Change oil in car | 45 |
| 6:15 - 6:30 | Clean up for supper | 15 |
| 6:30 - 7:15 | Supper and family devotions | 45 |
| 7:15 - 7:30 | Open mail | 15 |
| 7:30 - 8:35 | Review math with Tim | 65 |
| 8:35 - 8:50 | Finish handling mail | 15 |
| 8:50 - 9:25 | Begin sermon research | 35 |
| 9:25 - 10:15 | Crisis counseling via telephone | 50 |
| 10:15 - 10:20 | Prayer for crisis | 5 |
| 10:20 - 11:00 | Resume sermon research | 40 |

it. If you work, you may want to keep two different inventories: one for time on the job and the other for time on your own. These inventories should be kept for a minimum of one week and preferably for two weeks.

The next step is to categorize your time expenditures and add up how much you spent in each category. This is called a *cumulative time inventory*. For example, lump all of your exercise time, whether jogging or playing tennis (Exhibit 6-4). Add up the total time in all categories and check to see if it agrees with the total time available (168 hours in a week). The time in each category divided by the total is the percentage of your time spent in that activity.

Be prepared for a shock. You may be appalled at your skimpy devotional life. You may feel remorse about how little time you're spending with your family. Perhaps you will feel guilty about how much time you waste at the office. You may kick yourself for the time you spend mesmerized in front of the TV. Socrates said, "Know thyself. The unexamined life is not worth living."

Peter Drucker tells the story of a company president who claimed he divided his time into three parts. "I spend one-third of my time with my senior staff, one-third with important customers, and one-third in community activities." His time inventory revealed nothing of the kind. A time log taken over six weeks showed he spent almost *no* time in any of these areas. Actually, he spent most of his time as a kind of dispatcher—keeping track of orders from customers he knew personally and bothering the manufacturing plant with telephone calls about them. Most of these orders were going through all right anyhow; his intervention only served to delay them. He couldn't believe it (R. Moskowitz, *Total Time Management*, Amacon, tape 1).

A pastor who attended one of my time-management seminars, told the group he felt a daily quiet time was important. He said he tried to spend one hour each day in prayer and in the Word. Three weeks later, I happened to run into him and I asked if he had found the seminar practical. He told me that he had just completed a two-week time inventory and that it was a revelation. He sheepishly confessed, "My quiet times for one week totaled

## EXHIBIT 6-4  CUMULATIVE TIME INVENTORY*
### OUTSIDE OF WORK

| | | |
|---|---|---|
| Quiet time (including devotional Bible study and prayer) | 5¼ hours | 3.1% |
| Time at church (including travel time) | 8 hours | 4.8% |
| Bible study and sermon preparation | 20½ hours | 12.2% |
| Neighborhood Bible study (including preparation) | 2½ hours | 1.5% |
| Visitation (including evangelistic) | 5 hours | 3.0% |
| Family fun time (not including meals) | 5¼ hours | 3.1% |
| Time communicating with wife (including luncheon) | 3¾ hours | 2.2% |
| Helping boys with homework | 3 hours | 1.8% |
| Counseling | 5½ hours | 3.3% |
| Correspondence | 2 hours | 1.2% |
| Maintenance (car, house, and appliances) | 2½ hours | 1.5% |
| Exercise time (jogging and racquetball) | 3½ hours | 2.1% |
| Personal hygiene (shaving, showering, etc.) | 3½ hours | 2.1% |
| Sleeping | 45½ hours | 27.1% |
| Eating | 5½ hours | 3.3% |
| TV time | 1 hour | 0.5% |
| (Time at work) | 44½ hours | 26.5% |
| **TOTAL** | 166¾ hours | |
| **Unaccounted for** | 1¼ hours | 0.7% |
| *One week | | 100.0% |

less than one hour!" He hastened to add, "But it was an atypical week." I've often wondered when I could find a typical week.

I have yet to find a person who completed a time inventory and didn't learn something new about himself. I've seen housewives amazed at how much time they spend in the grocery store. Students who wondered where their time went found they consumed it in "bull sessions." A pastor's wife was appalled at the number of hours she spent on the telephone. A time inventory is essential for intelligent self-analysis.

## Analyzing Your Time Inventory

Take a hard look at each category on your *Cumulative Time Inventory* sheet, and the percentage of time spent in that activity. First take each category and identify which ones relate to your goals. You have already developed a list of three top goals which you numbered in order of priority. Take the goal number and place it beside each of the activities which support that particular goal on your *Cumulative Time Inventory*. Then ask yourself the following questions:

- Why did you do those things not associated with your goals?
    Someone asked you to?
    Interruption?
    Unexpected event?
    Enjoyable?
    Easiest course?
- Which items were *time wasters?*
    Can they be eliminated?
    Can they be delegated?
- Which tasks can be done more efficiently?
    Where can you use your time twice (e.g., praying while driving to work)?
- Are some of your goals obsolete?
- Should you establish new goals?

Obviously some activities not associated with our goals are legitimate. However, their legitimacy often means that they support one of our goals indirectly. But remember, the objective is to compare our goals (what we want to do) with our use of time (what we're actually doing).

Now, go back and establish a new set of categories related to the biblical priority grid discussed previously:
- God
- Immediate family
- Family of God
- Others

Each of these broad categories can be broken down into sub-categories related to your various activities.

## GOD
- Personal prayer time
- Reading the Bible
- Memorizing Scripture and meditating on it
- Reading Christian literature

## IMMEDIATE FAMILY
- Time with whole family (meals, travel, vacations)
- Time with spouse (meals with just the two of you, trips, sports, shopping, talking, making love)
- Time with kids (taking to school, helping with homework, supervising yard work or other chores, sports, games, talking)
- Family maintenance (laundry, dishes, house cleaning, yard work, paying bills, fixing house, getting car fixed)

## FAMILY OF GOD
- Time in church
- Time in small fellowship group
- Time preparing for talk
- Counseling
- Visitation
- Committee meetings
- Funerals or weddings
- Preaching, teaching, or leading

## OTHERS
- Employer

- Colleagues at work
- Neighbors
- Strangers
- Social service (schools, volunteer work)

If you have kept a time inventory for your work, you will need to see how efficiently you are using time on the job. A manager might categorize his activities as follows:

- Supervision time
- Meetings
- Planning
- Writing and reviewing reports
- Mail: in and out
- Telephone
- Reading and study

Don't forget yourself. Personal maintenance and development permits you to be more effective in ministering to others. You should have categories that cover personal hygiene (grooming, medical care, and sleep), physical exercise, hobbies, and just plain relaxation.

Still another way to assign categories uses the Luke 2:52 breakdown: intellectual, physical, spiritual, and social. Obviously, this breakdown overlaps some of the categories used above, but additional perspective may be gained by testing our inventory with Luke 2:52. You may discover, as I have (Exhibit 6-5), that you lack balance in one sphere of life. When I see an inventory like that, it moves me to action. You will shed new light on your analysis if you categorize your activities in different ways.

You should do a time inventory at least once a year and preferably every six months. In subsequent inventories, you may want to use categories already established to check off your use of time in each 15-minute increment (Exhibit 6-6). Unless your lifestyle or circumstances have changed dramatically, the categories will remain essentially the same. This method will save you time.

If you want to spend apoproximately $400, you can buy a time logger. The device has space for 20 different activities. Every time you stop doing one activity and switch to another, you press the appropriate button. The time logger will tally the elapsed time for

**EXHIBIT 6-5** CUMULATIVE TIME INVENTORY*
Categorized by Luke 2:52

**INTELLECTUAL (Wisdom)**

| | |
|---|---|
| Bible study and sermon preparation | 20½ hours |
| Helping boys with homework | 3 hours |
| 25% of time at work | 11 hours |
| TOTAL | 34½ hours |

**PHYSICAL (Stature)**

| | |
|---|---|
| Exercise time | 3½ hours |
| Personal hygiene | 3½ hours |
| Sleeping | 45½ hours |
| Eating | 5½ hours |
| TOTAL | 58 hours |

**SPIRITUAL (In favor with God)**

| | |
|---|---|
| Quiet time | 5¼ hours |
| Time at church | 8 hours |
| Bible study and sermon preparation | 20½ hours |
| Neighborhood Bible study | 2½ hours |
| TOTAL | 36¼ hours |

**SOCIAL (In favor with man)**

| | |
|---|---|
| Neighborhood Bible study | 2½ hours |
| Visitation | 5 hours |
| Family fun time | 5¼ hours |
| Time communicating with wife | 3¾ hours |
| Helping boys with homework | 3 hours |
| Counseling | 5½ hours |
| Correspondence | 2 hours |
| Maintenance | 2½ hours |
| 25% of time at work | 11 hours |
| TOTAL | 40½ hours |

*One week

each activity. There is even an *idle button* for wasted time or activities not included in the 20 categories. Press the *read button* and a display shows the total cumulative time for any activity. Likewise the *total button* will display the time expended for all events, including *idle*. You can save yourself the money by spending five minutes a day setting up a table and adding up the time in each category (as in Exhibit 6-6).

Though a time inventory is essential for seeing how our time is spent, it can also be discouraging. There's never enough time to do all we would like to do. (I can only hope there will be enough time in heaven to pursue some of my "back-shelf" interests.) The Lord Jesus did not do everything He could have done, but He did what His Father gave Him to do. Priorities are the key. It's not how much you do that counts, it's how much you *get done*. Nothing is easier than being busy, and nothing is more difficult than being effective.

A discouraging aspect of a time inventory is the wasted time it reveals—"the years that the locust hath eaten" (Joel 2:25, KJV). It is shocking to see how much of our lives go down the tube. Yet this revelation is the greatest benefit of a time inventory. We cannot eliminate a time bandit until we identify it.

A key question is, "What will happen if I stop doing this?" If the answer is *nothing*, stop doing it. Even one hour redeemed every day would amount to over three weeks of 16-hour days— more than my annual vacation. "So teach us to number our days, that we may apply our hearts unto wisdom." (Ps. 90:12, KJV).

## Take Action!

Do we really want to redeem the time? Are we willing to change our lifestyles to accomplish more for Christ? The problem with most of us is that we live our lives the way we watch TV. Even though the program is not as good as we would like, we're too lazy to get up and change it.

Why not begin now and construct a *hate list* of five things you would like to eliminate from your life. This should include activities which harm you intellectually, physically, spiritually, or socially; activities which compete for time you should be using to

**EXHIBIT 6-6** Work time log (Compare with 6-1)
Wednesday, February 24

| | REPORTS AND PRESENTATIONS | MAIL INCOMING | MAIL OUTGOING | MEET-INGS | SUPER-VISION | PLAN-NING | READING & STUDY | TELE-PHONE |
|---|---|---|---|---|---|---|---|---|
| 8:00 | X | | | | | | | |
| | X | | | | | | | |
| 8:30 | X | | | | | | | |
| | X | | | | | | | |
| 9:00 | X | | | | | | | |
| | X | | | | | | | |
| 9:30 | X | | | | | | | |
| | X | | | | | | | |
| 10:00 | X | | | | | X | | |
| | X | | | | | X | | |
| 10:30 | X | | | | | | | |
| | X | | | | | | | |
| 11:00 | X | | | | | | | |
| | X | | | | | | | |
| 11:30 | | | | | | | | X |
| | | | | | | | | X |
| 12:00 | | | | | | | | |
| | | | | | | | | |
| 12:30 | | | | | | | | |
| | | | | | | | | |
| 1:00 | | | | | | | | |
| | | | | | | | | |
| 1:30 | | X | | | | | | |
| | | X | | | | | | |
| 2:00 | | X | | | | | | |
| | | | X | | | | | |
| 2:30 | | | X | | | | | |
| | X | | | | | | | |
| 3:00 | | | | X | | | | |
| | | | | X | | | | |
| 3:30 | | | | X | | | | |
| | | | | X | X | | | |
| 4:00 | | | | X | X | | | |
| | | | | | | | X | |
| 4:30 | | | | | | | X | |
| | | | | | | | X | |
| 5:00 | | | | | | | X | |
| | | | | | | X | | |

pursue your major goals; and activities which are totally non-productive in terms of goals or benefits to others or yourself. Some unprofitable activities can't be avoided. Perhaps you can do these tasks with someone you need to spend time with; make it a game to enhance interpersonal relationships. You may also be able to combine these odious tasks with another activity which is more enjoyable, or which has higher productivity.

After you've completed your time inventory, your analysis, and your *hate list*, share them with your spouse or a close friend. See if they approve of how you're spending time. They may be able to help identify time wasters too.

# 7

# Time's a Wasting

I had a deadline. The project report was due in one week. I estimated that I could readily accomplish the 60 hours of work in the 7 days were it not for a trip to the East Coast to teach a 4-day course on membrane filtration technology. My only alternative was to take the report with me and work on it between sessions. I figured I could squeeze out just enough time to complete the report:

| | |
|---|---|
| Flight time to Newark | 5 hours |
| Monday evening | 5 hours |
| Tuesday evening | 5 hours |
| Wednesday evening | 5 hours |
| Thursday evening | 5 hours |
| Flight time to San Francisco | 5 hours |
| Saturday | 15 hours |
| Sunday | 15 hours |
| | 60 hours |

If I could work uninterrupted on the plane, and if I could excuse myself from long business dinners in the evenings, I projected that I could have the report ready for typing first thing Monday morning. I didn't like missing church but thought maybe I could complete the job ahead of schedule. I packed my brief case full of work associated with the report and put my slides and clothes in another large bag to check. Normally, I pack everything in a brief case and a small carryon to eliminate checking and retrieving baggage.

The plane was full, and because I was short on time, I got to the airport too late to select a good seat. I found myself sitting between a young mother with a six-month old baby and an elderly woman who loved to talk.

I wasted no time in getting out my report, but this did not discourage my matronly friend. She wanted to talk! She began with her grandchildren, discussed the marriages of three daughters, and talked about her late husband. I was curt and downright rude; I explained I had a deadline to meet on my report. She suggested we talk while I worked on it.

Meanwhile, the baby on my left began to cry. He was airsick, I think, because eventually he threw up on my report.

About this time, I gave up! I decided the Lord was telling me to talk to my matronly friend. Every time I tried to turn the conversation to the spiritual, she changed the subject. I finally blurted out, "Would you be ready to die if the plane crashed now?" Everybody turned and looked at me. The stewardess eyed me with suspicion. I was talking louder than I thought—above the baby's crying.

When I arrived in Newark I had completed only one page of the report (which had to be rewritten due to the accident) and the conversation seemed devoid of eternal value. I had to wait one hour for my luggage and another for a limo. When I arrived at the hotel it was 7 P.M. After a snack, I worked three hours on the report. I was already seven hours behind schedule.

The first day of the course went smoothly, but one of the participants insisted we go to dinner that evening to discuss a confidential project. I didn't get back to my room until 9 P.M. I had eaten too much and was so sluggish I couldn't think clearly enough to do the calculations needed for the report. I finished one page and went to bed early. I was then 11 hours behind schedule.

I reserved Wednesday night for the report. I refused all invitations to dinner and grabbed a hamburger instead, but I was so beat from the day of lecturing I decided to relax with the 6:30 news before I began to work. Following the news, I discovered *Patton* was the featured movie. I rarely watched TV at home, but I was so tired, I reasoned I wouldn't get much done on the report anyway. After the movie, I did squeeze in an hour on it. I was then 15 hours behind schedule and I knew there was no way I could meet the deadline—even with immunity from further interruptions and distractions. Thursday through Sunday brought so many interruptions, the time deficit only widened!

Could I have done better? Certainly. Some of the interruptions were beyond my control, but others were my choice. Some of the interruptions were products of previous bad decisions. In large measure, I had chosen to waste time.

If the decision to waste time was not within our domain, we would not be commanded to redeem the time. In fact, it is precisely because the "days are evil" (Eph. 5:16, KJV) that we are exhorted to redeem (buy back) wasted time. We are continually besieged by circumstances and temptations designed to obstruct our meaningful use of time. We need to resist time wasters.

## Identifying Time Wasters

A time waster is an activity which is not as productive as another we could be doing. Probably the easiest way to spot one is by comparison. When we have a choice of doing two or more jobs and we do the less important one, we are probably stuck with a time waster. It keeps us from doing the more productive activity. We see three types of time wasters in the Parable of the Sower.

The sower went out to sow his seed; and as he sowed, some fell beside the road, and it was trampled under foot, and the birds of the air ate it up. And other seed fell on rocky soil, and as soon as it grew up, it withered away, because it had no moisture. And other seed fell among the thorns, and the thorns grew up with it, and choked it out. And other seed fell into the good ground, and grew up, and produced a crop a hundred times as great (Luke 8:5-8). Jesus gave the primary application of this parable.

The seed is the Word of God. And those beside the road are those who have heard, then the devil comes and takes away the word from their heart, so that they may not believe and be saved. And those on the rocky soil are those who, when they hear, receive the Word with joy; and these have no firm root; they believe for a while, and in time of temptation fall away. And the seed which fell among the thorns, these are the ones who have heard, and as they go on their way, they are choked with worries and riches and pleasures of this life, and bring no fruit to maturity. And the seed in the good soil, these are the ones who have heard the Word in an honest and good heart, and hold it fast, and bear fruit with perseverance (Luke 8:11-15).

Sometimes we plant seed which is stolen by the birds before the seed gets a chance to sprout and take root. I call these "birds" *time bandits*. An example of a time bandit is the elderly woman who insisted on talking. Interruptions are for the birds; they rob us of our intended use of time. They are often generated by someone or something else, and are beyond our control. We need to try to wave off the birds.

Other times, the seed we sow sprouts, but it has difficulty taking root. The little root runs into a rock and as a result, the plant withers. We often run into hidden obstacles. Had we known about them, we would have taken another course of action. We can attempt to remove the rock, but this often means we have to start over. I call these "rocks" *time spoilers* because they reduce our productivity. An example is my eating too much for dinner, resulting in sluggishness and diminished productivity that night in the Newark hotel room.

Then there are the ever-present thorns. Any farmer or gardener has a continual battle against weeds. They take up space and draw nutrients from the soil. Our "thorns" are *time chokers* that squeeze out more productive use of our time. They are internal interruptions over which we have control.

My decision to watch TV at the hotel instead of to work on the report is an example. This was a "pleasure of life" which Jesus said sometimes chokes the Word like a thorn. He also mentioned worries and riches. Our material possessions can also become encumbrances (excess baggage).

## Jesus Eliminated Time Wasters

Was the Lord Jesus concerned about eliminating time wasters? You bet He was! Read His instructions to the Twelve (Luke 9:1-6) and to the Seventy (Luke 10:1-11) before He sent them out.

He instructed His disciples to wave off the birds. "Greet no one on the way" (Luke 10:4). In other words, don't let casual conversations and excessive socializing rob you of the time you should be spending preaching and healing. To avoid these time bandits, He instructed both the Twelve and the Seventy, "Whatever house you enter ... stay in that house, eating and drinking what they give you. Do not keep moving from house to house" (Luke 9:4; 10:5, 7). Moving from house to house, sampling the hospitality and cooking of various families, would be time consuming.

Excessive socializing can be a "thorn" as well as a "bird." It would have been all too easy for the pleasures of eating to choke the mission of the disciples. They were to serve others—not to be served. Their mission was to preach and heal; not to be guests. Tasting hospitality could be a time choker.

Further, Jesus instructed both groups to travel light lest their possessions be an encumbrance—another "thorn." "Take nothing for your journey, neither staff, nor a bag, nor bread, nor money; and do not even have two tunics apiece" (Luke 9:3). "Carry no purse, no bag, no shoes" (Luke 10:4). Having too many possessions is a worry; we're always losing them, looking for them, collecting them, and packing them. They consume time and energy from our lives.

Then there is the "rocky soil." Jesus advised His disciples to look for more fertile fields. "And as for those who do not receive you, as you go out from that city shake off the dust from your feet as a testimony against them" (Luke 9:5). "But whatever city you enter and they do not receive you, go out into its streets and say, 'Even the dust of your city which clings to our feet, we wipe off in protest against you'" (Luke 10:10-11). Jesus is saying that we don't always know whether the ground is rocky until we test it. The rocks may be hidden beneath a thin layer of soil. When we discover "rocky soil," we are told not to try to remove the "rocks," but to move on to more fertile fields. Time spoilers undermine our fruitfulness.

As long as the Lord Jesus was with His disciples, He helped them see and eliminate many time wasters. When He ascended to the right hand of God the Father, He sent the Holy Spirit in His place. He said, "The Helper, the Holy Spirit, whom the Father will send in My name, He will teach you all things" (John 14:26). "But when He, the Spirit of Truth comes, He will guide you into all the truth" (John 16:13). "And your ears will hear a word behind you, 'This is the way, walk in it,' whenever you turn to the right or to the left" (Isa. 30:21).

In our key passage on time management (Eph. 5:15-16), "making the most of your time" (v. 16) is related to "being filled with the Spirit" (v.18). Effective time management is walking "according to the Spirit" and not "according to the flesh" (Rom. 8:4). The contrast is made between getting drunk which is dissipation and being filled with the Spirit.

Dissipation is the squandering of time and resources. The man who is under the influence of alcohol is wasting time in the extreme.

Rod Sargent of the Navigators tells of his life as an alcoholic before meeting Christ. "By the time I was 24, I had reached what Yale University calls 'stage nine' in the life of an alcoholic. This stage is characterized by periods of mental blackout. The first time this happened to me was after I'd gone to a bar on Hollywood Boulevard. I could remember everything until 10 o'clock that night. The rest was totally blank—I could not remember what I had done, where I had gone, or how I had gotten home."

According to the National Council on Alcoholism, there are 7 million alcoholics in this country who still try to work. They cost industry over $10 billion annually in absenteeism and inefficiency.

We are told to be under the control of the Holy Spirit (Eph. 5:18) rather than liquid spirits. When a person allows the Spirit to control his life, he has eliminated his number-one time waster—a life dissipated on himself. A converted drunkard was asked, "Do you believe that Jesus changed water into wine?" "Yes," he replied. "I have seen Him change whiskey into groceries and gambling tickets into furniture and a broken-hearted wife into a radiant Christian. I have no difficulty believing He changed water into wine!" The Holy Spirit can root out the "thorns" from our lives. He can guide us away from "rocky soil." He can even shield us from the "birds."

Let's consider what can be done to control, minimize, and eliminate each type of time waster.

## Look Out for Time Bandits

Many of the participants in my time-management seminars do an excellent job setting goals, analyzing, and planning their use of time. The thing that blows them out of the saddle is the interruption over which they have no control.

A recent study of industrial executives showed none was able to work more than 20 minutes without an interruption. I have found from experience that this is a typical scenario: I sit down to work on a top priority project and a subordinate pops into my office to clarify his assignment. By the time he leaves, we have been interrupted three times by my telephone. At least one of the calls required immediate action. Another is my boss calling a meeting in one hour. With interruptions like these, what's the use in planning? It's like the farmer who plows his field and sows the seed, and then a huge flock of birds devours all the seed.

The amount of time wasted by interruptions is greater than it seems. The loss of momentum and train of thought can be recovered only with difficulty. "It was only a two-minute interruption," we say, but if we keep a record of interruptions and their duration, we will find that most of our time is wasted—not in hours but in minutes. Wasted time is like a leaky faucet. One drop per second can add up to 200 gallons down the drain each month.

What can be done about the "birds"? Martin Luther said, "I can't prevent the birds from flying over my head, but I can stop them from making a nest in my hair." Can anything be done about interruptions?

Take the drop-in visitor: Can a Christian justify being rude? I am commanded to "bear one another's burdens, and thus fulfill the Law of Christ" (Gal. 6:2). How can I do that and still get rid of the time bandit?

Some "birds" may be God-sent. Some birds drop the seed they devour on more fertile soil; in fact, some seeds won't germinate until they pass through the intestinal tract of a bird. How do we distinguish between time bandits and those whom God sends?

The first step is to pray for discernment. Second, pray that God will shield us from interruptions that keep us from His will. Third, learn how to discourage the time bandits without closing the door on opportunities. Here are some ideas that have helped me.

*Rearrange your office.* Remove extra chairs. I've noticed that the length of drop-in visits is directly related to the comfort of the visitor. Move your desk so you don't face the flow of traffic. Your front is more inviting than your side or back. Hang a large clock where it can be easily seen by your drop-in visitor. Remove such conversation pieces as photographs, paintings, and sculpture. These are nice, but they encourage lots of chit-chat.

Of course, conversation pieces can be used in reverse to stimulate witnessing opportunities. A book such as Chuck Colson's *Born Again* on your desk, may result in such an opportunity. Betsy Anker Johnson, a vice president of General Motors, has a sign on her wall: "One Maker ultimately recalls all of His products." If your gift is counseling, you may want drop-in visitors to feel comfortable, welcome, and invited. You may want to encourage small talk to put your visitors at ease. You must consider your goals and decide whether the arrangement of your office helps or hinders your effort to reach them.

*Close your door.* This may provide a small roadblock to those wanting to intrude on your time. It forces them to knock and in so doing ask the question, "May I interrupt?" I find a closed door effectively communicates that I don't want to be interrupted. Most of my colleagues respect this—except in emergencies.

The problem with an open-door policy is that you are always accessible to everybody. This means others will control how you spend your time. If you establish a regular time for the door to be closed, people will realize you are accessible at other hours and save their questions and comments until then.

*Learn to say* no. Be candid when someone asks, "Have you got a minute?" *No* is the most time-saving word in our vocabulary.

You can say it without being rude, particularly if you have a reputation for helping others, and if you're willing to schedule a time with the person later on, explaining why you're busy now. When you say *yes* to any request, you have in effect said *no* directly or indirectly to something else, possibly more important.

The telephone can be as much of a time bandit as the drop-in visitor. Ironically, it also can be one of your biggest time-savers. It is generally faster than a letter or a visit, but a jangling phone which frequently interrupts meetings or work on important projects can wipe out so-called saved time.

The trick is to control input calls so they don't become time bandits. A secretary or a family member can be a great help in screening and grouping calls. The idea is to group calls and return them at one time.

What about the caller who engages in endless small talk and trivia? You need to bring your calls to a prompt close by politely serving notice that you are ready to hang up. "Before we hang up, I'd like to . . ." is a tactful way of indicating you're finished with the conversation.

By the way, if a caller says he must see you as soon as possible, try to set up the meeting in his office instead of yours. You'll have more control over the length of the meeting. It's easier to get up and leave his office than your own.

At the very minimum, try to limit damage done by interruptions by jotting a note to yourself about what you're thinking or doing at the time of the interruption. This keeps you from losing your train of thought forever; it maintains momentum, reduces start-up time after the interruption, and it lets the interrupter know you are busy.

One more thing about time bandits, we must not be one ourselves. We should watch how we use the phone, and be sensitive about wasting other people's time. If we call meetings, we must make sure we are prepared, know what we want to accomplish, have an agenda, and set a time limit.

We must be particularly careful that we don't steal time from our bosses. Time thievery is a corporate crime that may cost U.S. business $120 billion this year, estimates management recruiter

Robert Half of Robert Half International, Inc., New York. Who are these corporate burglars? Employees who take unwarranted sick days, read newspapers and magazines on company time, conduct personal business during working hours, take unusually long lunch breaks, socialize excessively with co-workers, and routinely arrive late and leave early. Robert Half says that time theft per employee comes to a weekly average of 245 minutes, which is equivalent to 204 hours a year or over 25 eight-hour days. Of course, most employees waste far more than 49 minutes a day due to disorganization or lack of planning.

Preachers and teachers can be time bandits too. I believe the Lord will hold us accountable not only for living what we preach, but for the stewardship of our listener's time. The average attendance at our church is 500. I am particularly sensitive to the fact that a bad 45-minute sermon wastes 375 man-hours or over 23 man-days (16-hour days). "We who teach shall be judged with greater strictness" (James 3:1, RSV).

## Beware of Time Spoilers

Jesus instructed His disciples to move on to more fertile fields if their preaching was unproductive. The Lord can steer us away from the nonproductive fields if we are sensitive to His leading. The Spirit forbade Paul to preach in Asia and directed him to Macedonia instead (Acts 16:6-10).

In 1972 our growing family was beginning to crowd out our small home in Bedford, Massachusetts. My wife Carol was pushing to buy a bigger house. We knew the longer we waited, the more expensive a move would be.

Carol began to look for a larger house, and on weekends I looked with her. Every time we went a voice inside said, "You're wasting your time!" Later, Carol also confessed the same inward sense of futility on these house-hunting safaris.

On and on we looked, week after week, month after month. Nothing seemed right to us. I believe the Spirit of God graciously kept us from a big mistake, for in nine months an unforeseen job change resulted in our moving to California.

The exasperating job of house hunting in Massachusetts became almost effortless in California. In three days, we found an ideal five-bedroom house 10 minutes from my new job. We sold our Bedford home in less than a week. God was gracious, but we could have saved ourselves many weekends of house hunting in Massachusetts if we had paid attention to the promptings of the Spirit.

The well-known author, Agnes Sanford, had a similar experience. She had an important engagement in Richmond, Virginia, but several hours prior to her departure she was aware of a strong inner feeling telling her not to go. It didn't make sense so she disregarded it. Before the train reached Richmond, there was a wreck on the track ahead. The train stopped in time, but the passengers were forced to sit up all night waiting for the track to be cleared. "Afterward," Agnes said, "I realized that the inner voice had been trying to warn me of this" (Quoted by Catherine Marshall, *The Helper*, Word, p. 90).

"Therefore be careful how you walk, not as unwise men, but as wise, making the most of your time, because the days are evil. So then do not be foolish, but understand what the will of the Lord is" (Eph. 5:15-17). Only God's wisdom can help us overcome hidden obstacles (rocks). Sometimes He helps us get rid of them; sometimes He leads us around them.

Productivity can also be greatly influenced by timing. If seed is sown in the hot summer when there is little moisture in the surface soil and the sun scorches the plant, it will wither and die. On the other hand, if the seed is sown during the rainy season, the roots may have a chance to grow around the rocks into deeper soil. Doing work out of sequence may be totally nonproductive (like mopping the kitchen floor just before the kids come home from school on a rainy day). There are also times during the day when we can cope with complex tasks better than at other times. Timing can make the difference in whether or not we are productive.

God sometimes allows obstacles to teach us perseverance. "Let us not be weary in well doing: for in due season we shall reap, if we faint not" (Gal. 6:9, KJV). We recognize that the ground is cursed because of Adam's sin (Gen. 3:17) and that it will produce only with toil and sweat. Murphy's law is a direct result of the Fall: "If anything can go wrong, it will."

## We Choke Ourselves (Time Chokers)

Jesus said the thorns which choke us are the "cares and riches and pleasures of this life" (Luke 8:14, KJV). We have no one but ourselves to blame for these thorns. "For he that soweth to his flesh shall of the flesh reap corruption; but he that soweth to the Spirit shall of the Spirit reap life everlasting" (Gal. 6:8, KJV). We reap what we sow. If we sow for our own self-gratification, it will all come to nought. If we sow for the Spirit, what we accomplish will have eternal value.

This kind of weed continually infests our lives. The best soil in the world is not immune. Thorns are usually harmless in and of themselves. They become a problem because they choke out the more productive plants. When we have a choice of two or more things to plant, and we plant the worthless one, we have *chosen* a time choker.

The psalmist said, "I will set no worthless thing before my eyes. . . . It shall not fasten its grip on me" (Ps. 101:3). In *By Searching*, Isobel Kuhn told how she had to stop reading romantic novels because they were robbing her of time for God's work. Other diversions such as television, excessive socializing, or even the simple pleasures of life can be time chokers.

> The TV is my shepherd.
> It maketh me to sit down and
> do nothing for His Name's sake,
> because it requireth all
> my spare time.
>
> It restoreth my knowledge of
> the things of the world,
> and keepeth me from the
> study of God's Word.
> Its sound and picture
> they comfort me.

Yea, though I live to be 100,
I shall keep on viewing
as long as it works.
Surely no good thing
will come of my life.

Author unknown

Dr. Merril E. Douglass, director of the Time Management Center in Grandville, Michigan, has done research which shows that almost everyone wastes 2 hours every day by our own choice. (*Manage Your Time, Manage Your Work, Manage Yourself*, Amacom, p. 117). It is not that this time is beyond our control; it is because we *enjoy* wasting it. That's 730 hours (a month-and-a-half of 16-hour days).

Then there is the "deceitfulness of riches" (Mark 4:19, KJV). Some possessions may appear to be time savers but actually are time chokers when we consider maintenance and other factors.

A cluttered desk may come under the heading of "too many things." What is it that makes me reluctant to throw away things? It's probably related to my love for material things. Organizing my desk and staying on top of the paper flow is my most difficult battle. I find that clutter tends to expand to fill the space available. When we moved from a three-bedroom house to a five-bedroom house, it quickly filled with clutter.

Paperwork of all kinds can choke the flow of work and impair productivity. In *Getting Organized*, Stephanie Winston states that only three useful things can be done with a piece of paper: it can be thrown away, it can be acted upon as required, or it can be filed for reading or action at a more appropriate time. Too often we shuffle and reshuffle papers from pile to pile with no action. Winston's crucial point is that *we must act* on each piece of paper. We should form the habit of making a decision each time we pick up a piece of paper (Warner Books, p. 65).

Jesus referred to worry as a "thorn" too. Often we worry about our possessions—how to keep them or find them. Worry deprives us of sleep and saps our energy. One woman lamented, "No wonder I'm worn out. I do everything three times. First, I worry about doing it. Then I do it; and after I do it, I do it over, worrying about whether I did it right."

Worry can paralyze us. Jesus said, "Don't worry at all then about tomorrow. Tomorrow can take care of itself! One day's trouble is enough for one day" (Matt. 6:34, PH). The biblical antidote for worry is, "Be anxious for nothing, but in everything by prayer and supplication with thanksgiving let your requests be made known to God. And the peace of God, which surpasses all comprehension, shall guard your hearts and your minds in Christ Jesus" (Phil. 4:6-7). The key is to commit your concerns to the Lord and do it with thanksgiving.

See if you can identify "birds, rocks, and thorns" among these time wasters:

ON THE JOB

1. Lack of organization (poor filing system, no pocket calendar, lack of planning)
2. Putting off filing (means wasted time in looking for lost items)
3. Clutter (not returning things to their proper places or allowing paper to accumulate)
4. Being overly neat or organized (spending too much time cleaning and rearranging desk)
5. Too many meetings (A Danish device called an "econometer" automatically computes the total cost on a minute-by-minute basis factoring in the salary of all participants. Installed in the conference room, it operates like an electricity meter; the higher the rate of expenditure, the faster the disk rotates. The meter goes up to $10,000.00. Some meetings cost three times as much as the savings that result from the decisions made at the meeting.)
6. Handling trivial assignments while keeping the big job on hold
7. Delving into aspects of the job which don't concern us
8. Doing everything anybody asks us to do (never saying no)
9. Doing something that could be delegated, such as work beneath our capabilities (executives spend 35 percent of

their time performing secretarial or clerical tasks) or work way over our heads (pride keeps us from going to someone more qualified)

10. Doing what someone else has already done (reinventing the wheel)
11. Excessive socializing or small talk (a form of escape)
12. A heavy lunch (makes you sluggish, even sleepy, in the afternoon; try the salad bar)
13. Writing a letter when a phone call will do
14. Uncontrolled interruptions (taking any call any time and maintaining an open-door policy)
15. Perfectionism (not knowing when to stop)
16. Analysis paralysis (immobility caused by substituting study for courage)
17. Waiting until the last moment before a deadline (automatically increases the chances of mistakes and having to do it over)
18. Delaying decisions (unless we are waiting for more information) means we will take more and more time to decide

FOR HOMEMAKERS (in addition to above)

1. TV soap opera
2. Telephone chitchat
3. Socializing with other homemakers over coffee (unless we can direct this toward evangelism)
4. Saying *yes* to every request ("Yes, I'll sew eight angel costumes for the church pageant.")
5. Failing to plan meals
6. An upset household (Someone who is irritated or mad at another person accomplishes little else.)
7. Shopping without a list (Lapses in memory mean additional trips.)

I know a manager of engineering who bought himself a large six-inch wooden letter Q. He uses it as a paperweight on his desk to remind him to ask himself, "Is this the best use of my time right now?" Many of his drop-in visitors ask him what the Q is for. His explanation makes the visitor less inclined to waste the manager's time and more inclined to start a time-management program for himself.

Here are seven questions designed to keep away time bandits, to avoid time spoilers, and to control time chokers.

- Is this the best use of my time right now?
- What's being neglected while I do this?
- What will happen if this never gets done?
- Who can do this better than myself?
- Is this the best time to do this?
- Have I done what I can to minimize interruptions?
- Is this a Spirit-sent interruption?

# 8

# How to Find Time You Never Knew You Had

Russell Conwell was the successful pastor of the Baptist Temple in Philadelphia (1891-1925). One day, a group of young men asked him if he would be willing to instruct them in college courses; they wanted the education, but lacked the money to pay for it. Conwell was so intrigued with the idea of founding a college for poor but deserving young men, he became the founder and first president of Temple University (1888-1925).

Dr. Conwell raised $7 million to start the school. He did so by giving more than 6,000 lectures throughout the country. In each of them he told a true story called "Acres of Diamonds."

The story was the account of an African farmer who heard tales of settlers making millions by discovering diamond mines. These tales so excited the farmer that he sold his farm and spent the rest of his life wandering over the vast African continent searching unsuccessfully for diamonds. Finally, in a fit of despondency, broke and desperate, he threw himself into a river and drowned.

Meanwhile, the man who bought his farm found a large and unusual stone in a stream which cut through the property. The stone turned out to be a great diamond of enormous value. He soon discovered other diamonds on the farm property. It became one of the world's richest diamond mines.

The first farmer had owned acres of diamonds, but had sold

them for practically nothing in order to look for them elsewhere. If he had only taken the time to explore and analyze his own property, he would have found what he sought.

The thing about this story that so profoundly affected Dr. Conwell and those who attended his lectures was the idea that each of us is standing in the middle of an acre of diamonds. People are always complaining about how busy they are and saying, "If only I had the time he does, I could. . . ." In reality we all have hidden blocks of time waiting to be discovered and put to use.

## An Inexhaustible Resource

It is when time is exhausted and the deadline is upon us that God says, "My grace is sufficient for thee."

One Saturday, I was in a time bind to prepare a sermon for the next day. The previous week had been packed with meetings and business engagements. I realized I would have to do with less than the usual 20 hours I allocate for preparing a sermon. I prayed that God would help me redeem the time and give me direction in organization and content. I prayed that He would free me from interruptions.

No sooner had I prayed than my wife interrupted with a distress call from the kitchen. The dishwasher was overflowing water onto the kitchen floor. It took three hours to locate the problem and replace the rubber diaphragm in the solenoid valve. Then it was time for lunch.

I returned to my study and was able to put in three hours before the next interruption. It was a phone call from a brother in crisis; he wanted me to come right over for counsel and prayer. How could I refuse? Jesus would not have put him off. I managed to get back in time for a late supper.

After supper my oldest son asked for help on a science project. "Could we put it off until tomorrow afternoon?" I asked. "No!" The youth group had an outing all day Sunday and the project was due Monday.

Two hours later I returned to my study in a bit of a panic. I had only a few hours left. I prayed for a miracle!

Has time ever stopped for you? It did for me that night.

The hands of the clock seemed to stand still! It was as though 3 hours became 10. Psychological delusion? Perhaps. Nevertheless, the effective time at my disposal was more than the clock measured.

It is experiences like this which have prompted me to examine more carefully the experience of Joshua. The kings of the Amorites had besieged Gibeon; they sent a call for help to Joshua, and the Lord assured him of victory. But Joshua ran out of time; dusk was fast approaching, and the enemy was not yet destroyed. Joshua spoke to the Lord and asked for the sun to stand still "until the nation avenged themselves of their enemies" (Josh. 10:12-13). For years, scientists and theologians have debated what happened. The bottom line was that Joshua got the extra time he needed. Is this so remarkable when you consider that God is the Creator of time? "One day is with the Lord as 1,000 years, and 1,000 years as one day" (2 Peter 3:8 KJV).

I do not believe God will compensate for my abuse of time. He will not make up for two hours spent in front of the one-eyed monster or for the hour of meaningless chitchat on the telephone, but He will make up for the hour spent in crisis counseling and the trip to the hospital to visit a sick friend. "Give, and it shall be given unto you" (Luke 6:38, KJV) seems to apply to time as well as money.

The Lord Jesus laid down one basic principle of discipleship—a paradox. "Whoever wishes to save his life shall lose it; and whoever loses his life for My sake and the Gospel's shall save it" (Mark 8:35). Perhaps we can rephrase this to read, "Whoever wishes to save time shall lose it; and whoever loses his time for My sake and the Gospel's shall save it." There are a lot of time nuts who are spinning their wheels rushing hither and yon to save time, but "he who believes will not be in haste" (Isa. 28:16, RSV).

Jesus Christ was the greatest time-management expert the world has seen. He did not frantically rush here and there to redeem the time. His was the life of faith. He was careful to walk in God's plan and leave the results with Him.

## Ways to Redeem Time

If you have completed your time inventory and asked, "Why am I doing things not associated with God's goals for my life?" you are well on your way to finding acres of lost diamonds.

Three techniques which will help us "redeem the time" are fill the spaces, double up, and delegate.

*Fill the Spaces.* C. H. Spurgeon gave the following illustration in one of his sermons: "Select a large box, and place in it as many cannon balls as it will hold, and it is, after a fashion, full; but it will hold more if smaller matters can be found. Bring a quantity of marbles; very many of these may be packed in the spaces between the larger globes. The box is now full, but still only in a sense; it will contain more yet. There are spaces in abundance, into which you may shake a considerable quantity of small shot, and now the chest is filled beyond all question; but yet there is room. You cannot put in another shot or marble, much less another ball, but you will find that several pounds of sand will slide down between the larger materials, and, even then between the granules of sand, if you empty yonder jug, there will be space for all the water, and for the same quantity several times repeated. Where there is no space for the great, there may be room for the little; where the little cannot enter, the less can make its way: and where the less is shut out, the least of all may find ample room. So where time is, as we say, fully occupied, there must be stray moments, occasional intervals, and bits of time which might hold a vast amount of little usefulness in the course of months and years."

We must be good stewards of the stray moments in our lives as well as the hours. "He who is faithful in a very little thing is faithful also in much" (Luke 16:10). A sign in a colleague's office reads: "Five minutes is a long time."

John Erskine, well-known author, professor, and lecturer, says he learned the most valuable lesson of his life when he was 14. His piano teacher asked him how long at a stretch he practiced. He replied that he practiced for an hour or more at a time. "Don't do that," warned the teacher. "When you grow up, time won't come in long stretches. Practice in minutes, whenever you can find them—5 or 10 before school, after lunch, between chores. Spread the practice throughout the day, and music will become a part of your life" (*Bits and Pieces*, Economic Press, June, 1981).

Erskine said this advice enabled him to live a comparatively complete life as a creative writer, outside his regular duties as an instructor. "Whenever I had 5 free minutes, I wrote 100 words or so. To my astonishment, at the end of the week I had a sizeable manuscript ready for revision. Later I wrote novels by the same piecemeal methods." He wrote most of *Helen of Troy*, his most famous work, on streetcars while commuting between his home and the university.

It was amid rattling newspapers and smoke-filled air that Ken Taylor put together the whole of *The Living Bible* while riding the commuter train between Wheaton and Chicago. Well over 25 million copies of this paraphrase have been distributed. A by-product was the beginning of Tyndale House, a successful Christian publishing firm.

A friend learned a whole new language over a period of a year using 30 minutes each day on a commuter train. And David Cornwell, while traveling on a commuter train in England, scribbled in little notebooks instead of gazing at the scenery. When his scribblings were typed, a publisher bought them and they became the best-selling novel *The Spy Who Came In From The Cold* by John LeCarre (Cornwell's pen name).

It is said that in a lifetime every person spends more than a year waiting: waiting in the checkout line, for planes, for the car to be fixed, at the barber shop, in the doctor's office, or for a spouse. Few of us enjoy waiting, but some of us use the time better than others. The Lord Jesus, while waiting for His disciples to bring food, talked to the woman at the well. The result was the Samaritan revival. While waiting for Martha to prepare the meal, He used the time to teach Mary.

In *Prayer—The Mightiest Force in the World*, Frank Laubach speaks of "the game with minutes"— using minutes between events to pray (Revell, pp. 51-69). We can pray for pedestrains or motorists while we wait for traffic lights to change. After dialing the phone we can pray for the person we're calling. We can use the time in the doctor's waiting room to pray for other patients. Next time you are waiting for the elevator, for the toast to pop, or for the bathtub to drain, pray. These wasted moments can be put to great and powerful use for the kingdom.

George Cowan, past president of the Wycliffe Bible Translators, once said, "I believe television commercials are a gift of God, especially those that come on during the evening news. Invariably there's something in each news segment that calls for prayer. Maybe it's the international situation, or government officials, or some tragedy in a person's life. When the commercial comes on, we pray about what we've just seen." Maybe Laubach and Cowan have discovered what Paul meant when he said, "Pray without ceasing" (1 Thes. 5:17, KJV).

A college professor once told his graduating class, "I hope when you are married and your wife tells you she is almost ready except for a couple of last-minute touches, you will sit down and read a book. You will be surprised at how much knowledge you will acquire." Dick Schneider, an editor for *Guideposts*, insists that he read the whole Great Books Library over the years while waiting for his wife to get ready.

Most Christians know that by spending 10 minutes a day, they can read through the whole Bible in a year. Or that by spending 15 minutes a day they can read 25 books in a year. Yet, few do it. I try to carry a paperback with me wherever I go. Unforseen spare moments often enable me to finish a book a week.

Some women make up a waiting kit to take with them. It might include a book, a notebook, envelopes with stamps, sewing or knitting. My wife often knits, or writes notes to friends while traveling or waiting. She goes prepared because she knows the value of five minutes here and five minutes there. Napoleon said he conquered the Austrians because they did not know the value of five minutes.

Short articles are great as transition projects. If we finish a three hour project a few minutes before lunch and have another two hour project scheduled for the afternoon, it's usually not efficient to begin the second project before lunch. We will only have to stop, and it will take extra time after lunch to find our place and recollect our thoughts.

## Doing Two Things at Once

*Double Up.* There is an adage which says, "You can't do two things at once," but the truth is you can and you should. We combine activities all the time. We walk and talk, eat and listen, drive and think.

Obviously, if an activity is automatic or involuntary, there is no conflict. On the other hand, two activities which require decisions and/or understanding ideas can never be automatized. Walking becomes automatic with practice, but comprehension does not.

William Hirst, Ulric Neissen, and Elizabeth Spilke of Cornell University have done extensive experiments on training people to read while writing sentences dictated to them. They found that students could learn to read an article in an encyclopedia with excellent comprehension, while writing sentences dictated to them, with very few errors and good recall ("Divided Attention," *Human Nature*, June 1978, pp. 54-61).

When I say double up, I'm not suggesting that we read while we take dictation, but these findings illustrate the potential in the human mind. A doubling up within the capability of each of us is what I call eyes-and-hands time. Experts say that even the busiest person has over 500 hours in a year when only his eyes and hands are busy (driving the car, dressing, showering, eating). If we use those 500 hours to learn something through our ears and minds, that's the equivalent of 10 semester courses at college. For example, we can listen to cassette tapes or the news with total concentration while driving to work, showering, or shaving. Any activity which is automatic or involuntary can be made more profitable by doubling up. Jesus was always doubling up. He used the time walking to the next town to teach His disciples—not to mention their mealtimes.

Passive activities are even easier to double up. When the barber cuts our hair, our hands are free, along with our eyes, to read a book or journal. Jesus caught up on His sleep while crossing the Sea of Galilee in a boat.

It works in reverse too. My wife cleans the kitchen counters and sink while she's on the phone (get a long cord). When the phone call is over, so is a job in the kitchen. A housewife can do lots of mini-jobs while she's talking on the phone. A list of mini-jobs near the telephone will remind you to double up—to clean a drawer, stack the dishwasher, or clean the oven while talking.

Why not make a list of your jobs which require no concentration. Then ask yourself what mental activity you can accomplish while doing them. For example: I jog over the same course every day; it's automatic. Can I pray or memorize verses while I jog? Yes! It enriches my jogging immensely. One woman I know prays for each member of her family as she cleans their respective rooms. It's the routine that makes it possible. A college student working in a cafeteria prays while she wipes tables. The more fervent her prayers, the harder she scrubs, until the tables are gleaming.

Habits are automatic actions which take no thought. Good habits are silent helpers. Organized people have established a force of good habits and live by a routine. If you do routine daily tasks (like shaving, showering, jogging, and eating) at the same time every day, the pattern you establish will eliminate decision time and permit doubling up with other mental activities. In *Psychocybernetics*, Dr. Maxwell Maltz writes that it takes 21 days to change a habit. He has proven that an idea must be repeated for 21 consecutive days before it becomes permanently fixed in the subconscious (*Psychocybernetics*, Prentice Hall, Preface).

## Why Delegate?

You are limited in what you can do yourself, but if you work through others you are unlimited. Some Christians view delegation as trying to push off their own work on others. It is viewed suspiciously as the selfish use of other people's time—an escape from personal responsibility. Yet anyone who studies the life of Christ will see that He delegated, giving others the privilege of participating, stimulating their growth, and extending His ministry.

The major goal of discipleship is to reproduce our lives and ministries in others. That's delegation. It multiplies our effectiveness through the lives of others. Jesus delegated authority to His disciples. He taught them to pray and preach the Gospel in His name (His authority). He made them a part of His ministry. He sent them into the village to inquire for food and lodging. He directed them to the city to prepare the Upper Room. But He also sent them forth as His ambassadors to preach and heal.

Jesus completed His mission in three-and-a-half years—even though He left thousands who had never heard the Gospel. He would not have completed His mission if He had not delegated the ongoing task to His disciples. "As Thou didst send Me into the world, I also have sent them into the world" (John 17:18). He told His disciples, "He who believes in Me, the works that I do shall he do also, and greater works than these shall he do; because I go to the Father" (John 14:12).

"If I want it done right, I'll have to do it myself." It is the height of pride to assume that nobody can do the job as well as I can. A refusal to delegate deprives others of a chance to get in on a ministry. If we insist on doing everything ourselves, our careers and our ministries will always be "stuck" at the present level.

Delegation leverages our time. Other people are the fulcrum; we are the force on the lever. We can move projects faster through greater distances depending on how close we get to our people (the fulcrum). Jesus developed an intimate relationship with 12 men who turned the world upside down.

Moses made the mistake of trying to lead the people of Israel by himself. He spent morning until evening judging the people—settling disputes and giving guidance. "Moses' father-in-law said to him, 'What you are doing is not good. You and the people with you will wear yourselves out, for the thing is too heavy for you; you are not able to perform it alone'"(Ex. 18:17-18, RSV). Jethro counseled Moses to "choose able men" to whom this ministry could be delegated. Hard cases were still referred to Moses, but it was easier for him because his delegates bore the burden with him. Moses followed his father-in-law's advice and was able to endure.

Naturally, the effectiveness of the program hinged on how able the men were. Jethro said they should be trustworthy men who feared God (v. 21), who were available (v. 22), and teachable (they brought great matters to Moses). In other words, they were

"F-A-T men" (faithful, available, and teachable). In the process, Moses trained his delegates (disciples) and helped them grow in responsibility.

The same discipling process is followed throughout the Bible. Paul wrote to a disciple, "The things which you have heard from me ... these entrust to faithful men, who will be able to teach others also" (2 Tim. 2:2).

Any parent knows we do our children a disservice if we do not delegate chores and responsibilities to them. They need to learn to maintain their rooms and clean up after themselves. They grow in the process.

Someone has said, "Never do anything someone else can or will do when there is so much others cannot or will not do." When properly done, delegation can be the means of channeling the efforts of everybody into a project in the most effective manner possible. I may be called upon to serve in a capacity which does not correspond to my spiritual gift. If I delegate the job to someone who is so gifted, I free myself for jobs which are compatible with my gift. This works even in the practical areas of everyday living. I delegate some jobs to my wife (who is far more adept at cooking and shopping) and she delegates some to me (like fixing the dishwasher). "Don't act thoughtlessly, but try to find out and do whatever the Lord wants you to" (Eph.5:17, LB).

Questions to ask yourself about any task:
- Who else can do this?
- Can they do it better?
- What would be a better use of my time?
- Is it my pride that keeps me from delegating?
- Is it my perfectionism that keeps me from delegating?
- Would it help someone to have this delegated responsibility?

One pastor felt bogged down in his ministry. For one thing, he never seemed to have enough time to pray for the church. He decided to go to all the infirm people in his church (the invalids, bedfast, elderly, and retired) and solicit their prayers for the church. He gave them books and articles on prayer. He established an

"Aaron and Hur Society" (Ex. 17:10-13) among these people. He reported, "With all that harnessed prayer, everything changed for the better. People who had fallen away came back. Women who hadn't talked to each other for years became friends. Many accepted Christ." That's effective delegation!

Look at this list of time savers and see if filling the spaces, doubling up, or delegating is involved.

ON THE JOB
  1. Get organized (use the DIP system):
     • Desk—reserve only for items needing immediate attention today.
     • Incoming box—for items which should be done this week.
     • Pile—for items to be done eventually
  2. Maintain a good filing system. (This will reduce the time it takes to find items; the purpose of a filing system should be to retrieve something, not store it.)
     • Reserve one set of files near your desk for the 20 percent of your work that takes up 80 percent of your time.
     • Other files are for the 80 percent of your work that demands only 20 percent of your attention.
  3. Develop a good memory, using association techniques. (This will help you remember where you filed something and may even obviate the necessity for filing.)
  4. When you read, underline or highlight. (This helps in retrieving information from books you've read. In just a few minutes you can grasp the central ideas of an entire book.)
  5. Learn a form of shorthand for taking notes.
  6. Avoid meetings where you are not needed or can't contribute. (Sometimes we are invited only as a courtesy.)
  7. Tackle toughest assignments first. (It's easy to procrastinate on tough assignments; do them while you're fresh and enthusiastic. You can do the more interesting projects even when fatigued.)
  8. Overcome fatigue with variety. (Switch to another task of equal priority for a stimulus change; a change in subject matter is often as good as a work break.)
  9. Overcome fatigue with an action break. (Walk briskly around

the office, get on an exercise bike, jog in place. Getting more oxygen enriched blood to your muscles will combat fatigue and increase mental clarity.)

10. Save repetitive and tedious paperwork for late in the day.

11. Handle each piece of paper only once. (Dispose of it before you put it down by responding, delegating, or filing. When in doubt throw it out. Shuffling paper is the inverse of doubling up.)

12. Learn to say *no* to activities which divert you from top goals.

13. Delegate everything you can.

14. Schedule a quiet hour for uninterrupted work with no phone calls or appointments (shut office door).

15. Have your secretary take your calls. Return them at one time.

16. If interrupted, try to maintain momentum by:
   • jotting a note to yourself of what you're thinking or doing before handling the interruption;
   • cutting out socializing.

17. Keep an "interruption log." (This will help you learn how often you're interrupted, when, and especially by whom. This way you can identify your main time wasters.)

18. Use your commute time effectively by:
   • riding public transportation if you need reading time;
   • driving later or earlier than rush hour;
   • listening to cassette tapes, memorizing Scripture, or praying while driving.

FOR HOMEMAKERS (in addition to above)

1. Don't be glued to the tube. (Limit yourself to a few programs of merit each week; don't flop down and watch whatever comes on. If you can't discipline your time here, give away the set.

2. Limit most phone calls to 3 minutes. (Keep a 3-minute egg-timer next to the phone.)

3. Double up with mini kitchen jobs while on the phone.

4. Where possible use labor saving devices. (But remember, "From everyone who has been given much shall much be required" [Luke 12:14].)

5. Recover lost items with prayer. (Spend one or two minutes praying. God will tell you where it is; then look the first place that comes to mind.)

6. Accumulate and organize errands. (Carry an envelope in your purse; list errands on outside and put related ads and lists inside.)

7. Check out stores by using yellow pages.

8. Group medical and dental appointments for two or more children.

9. Plan routing for errands. (When you have accumulated enough to warrant the time and gas, number in geographical sequence. Use the great circle route.)

10. Grocery shop no more than once a week. (Keep a list during the week and invite family members to add to the list.)

11. Schedule grocery shopping to avoid peak hours. (Experiment to find least crowded day and time—usually early in the week at 6 P.M. or 8 A.M. to 9 A.M. on weekends. Store managers often use these lulls to restock produce, so you have a better selection as well.)

12. Draw up and make copies of a master shopping list of all food and household items you buy at least once a month (preferably conforming to the layout of your favorite store). This way, instead of writing out a list each week, you simply check off the items you need.

13. Entertain simply. (Guests enjoy a relaxed barbeque or buffet more than a tense seven-course dinner. If you scale down the formality of your entertaining, it takes less time, and your guests will be relieved and do the same when they return the favor.)

14. Use the mail to pay bills and do banking.

TRAVEL TIPS

15. Make your plans directly with a travel agent. (This will save several phone calls.) Avoid going through your secretary. (You can explain what you want to the travel agent in less time.)

16. Carry your luggage onto the plane. (One under-the-seat bag for clothes and one brief case for papers and books is sufficient for even three weeks on the road. You will save much time in baggage claim areas and avoid lost bags.)

17. Park your car in the valet lot and be driven to the airport. (This avoids the one-mile walk from parking lot Z; pick up is faster too.)

18. Carry both heavy and light work projects with you. (Long flights are uninterrupted times to get heavy projects out of the way; light work is ideal for waiting rooms and ticket lines.)

MISCELLANEOUS

1. Be selective in your reading. (Learn to skim or file for future reference.)

2. Read 50,000 words a minute! (How? If not priority reading, skim the table of contents only.)

3. Skim newspaper headlines. (Resist the temptation to become immersed in the news; it is possible to be tuned into what is happening without knowing all the details.)

4. Better yet, listen to a newscast while shaving or commuting to work.

5. Institute a daily exercise program (e.g., jogging) to shorten sleep requirements and reduce sickness.

6. Think about puzzling questions just before retiring. (This allows your subconscious mind to work on the problem while you sleep; record the answer in the morning.)

Have you found extra time? Think of the time you spend reading this book as an investment. If, as a result, you save even 30 minutes a day, you will add the equivalent of 11 16-hour days to your life every year. At this rate, those who are 40 will add one full year to their lives. That's not a bad return on your investment.

# Section III
# PLANNING

# 9

# Fail to Plan?
# Plan to Fail!

In the early 1900s Charles Schwab, president of Bethlehem Steel Company, challenged Ivy Lee, a management consultant, with a problem faced by every aggressive businessman. "If you can show us a way to get more done, and it works, I'll pay you whatever you ask—within reason." Lee said he thought he could show Schwab a method that would increase his personal efficiency and that of his staff by at least 50 percent.

Ivy Lee suggested a four-point plan:

1. Write down the six most important tasks you should do tomorrow.

2. Number them in the order of importance.

3. First thing tomorrow morning, look at item number one and work on it until it's finished. Then tackle item number two the same way, then item number three, and so on.

4. Do this until quitting time. Don't be concerned if you have finished only one or two, because you will have done the most important projects. The others can wait until tomorrow.

Lee suggested that Schwab use the system until he had convinced himself and his staff of its value. "Then send me your check for whatever you think it's worth."

Within a few weeks, Charles Schwab sent a check made out to Ivy Lee for $25,000. Later Schwab commented, "This lesson was the most profitable of my entire business career." It helped make Bethlehem Steel the biggest independent steel producer in the world, and the leading manufacturer of war materials for the Allies in World War I. It helped Charles Schwab make a personal fortune of $100 million. Lee's method has been used in one form or another by thousands of people interested in time management. It is at the heart of the daily planning process.

Successful businessmen and management consultants are in universal agreement: planning and scheduling are essential. If you fail to plan, you have planned to fail. To make *no plans* is a plan in itself. David Jaquith, president of Vega Industries, has said, "Good results without good planning come from good luck, not good management." Crawford Greenwalt, former president of DuPont, has said, "One minute spent in planning saves three to four minutes in execution."

In one company study, two similar groups of projects were compared with respect to the time spent in planning and execution. Even though the planning process was twice as long for the second group, the total project time (including planning) was reduced by over 15 percent. In addition, the second group netted better results.

Every housewife knows that meal planning eliminates many trips to the store, reduces preparation time, minimizes cost, and provides a better balanced diet. In almost every area of life, planning makes the difference in results and time expenditures. Effort without planning is like continuing to chop wood without stopping to sharpen the axe.

Yet many Christians are uncomfortable with the whole concept of planning. They say, "Planning is unspiritual; it denies the Holy Spirit freedom to act."

## Is Planning Unspiritual?
Did you ever have that uneasy feeling that you have *planned* the Holy Spirit right out of it? Sometimes we seem to rely so much on forecasts and planning tools that God is left out. Let's face it; planning can be presumptuous and an affront to God. James seems to rebuke those who make elaborate business plans for tomorrow.

"You ought to say, 'If the Lord wills, we shall live and also do this or that' " (James 4:15). Yet a careful look at the passage shows that James is not condemning planning per se but *presumptuous* planning that assumes we control our destiny.

The Lord Jesus said, "Take therefore no thought for the morrow: for the morrow shall take thought for the things of itself" (Matt. 6:34, KJV). This implies to some that Jesus was against planning. However, a careful look at the context shows that Jesus is here dealing with worry rather than planning. Both the RSV and NASB translate verse 34, "Do not be anxious about tomorrow." And one of the ways we avoid worrying about tomorrow is to prayerfully plan ahead and leave the results with God.

Still another Scripture reference that seems anti-planning is Matthew 10:19-20, "But when they deliver you up, take no thought how or what ye shall speak: for it shall be given you in that same hour what ye shall speak. For it is not ye that speak, but the Spirit of your Father which speaketh in you" (KJV). That has to be the way to preach! What a time-saver—to be able to go into the pulpit without preparation and think nothing of it. I tried it a couple of times and found the congregation thought nothing of it too!

I later noticed a marginal note in the Scofield Reference Bible for Matthew 10:19 which says, "An instruction to martyrs, not to preachers." A more appropriate Scripture for preachers is 2 Timothy 2:15, "Study to show thyself approved unto God, a workman that needeth not to be ashamed, rightly dividing the Word of truth" (KJV). If the Holy Spirit can give martyrs the words to say on the spur of the moment, then surely He can also guide in the quietness of my study. Planning is responding to God's guidance in the most effective manner.

Those who make spiritual objections to planning forget that God Himself is the master planner. "For I know the plans I have for you, says the Lord, plans for welfare and not for evil, to give you a future and a hope" (Jer. 29:11, RSV). He sent His messenger to prepare for the coming of His Son (Mark 1:2-3). He planned and arranged for Caesar's decree to coincide with Mary's delivery so that Jesus would be born in Bethlehem, fulfilling the prophecy of Scripture (Micah 5:2).

It is also clear that Jesus had a plan for His own ministry; He seemed to operate with a schedule in view. At the very beginning of His ministry, He preached in Capernaum where He healed many. The next morning, His disciples impatiently interrupted His morning prayertime to tell Him: "Everyone is searching for You!" Jesus replied, "Let us go on to the next towns, that I may preach there also; for that is why I came out" (Mark 1:37-38, RSV). He was ever conscious of His timetable. "I must work the works of Him that sent Me, while it is day: the night cometh, when no man can work" (John 9:4, KJV).

Moses and Elijah spoke with Him on the Mount of Transfiguration of the plans for His departure (Luke 9:30-31). He was well aware of the divine plan and informed His disciples: He would be rejected by the religious leaders, be put to death, and after three days rise again (Mark 8:31).

On His last journey, we see Him headed for Jerusalem (Luke 9:51). He knew death was near, but He still had work to do. He preached in 35 towns and villages in Galilee, Samaria, Perea, and Judea. He planned the itinerary so He would arrive in Jerusalem in time for the Passover—to die on schedule in accordance with the 70-week prophecy of Daniel 9. He planned ahead for the Last Supper. He planned for His disciples to continue His mission. And at the end He reported to His Father that He had accomplished His plan (John 17:4). When they came to arrest Him, He offered no resistance; His hour had come! They had attempted to arrest Him before and even stone Him, but He always escaped. Why? Everything went according to plan.

Through the centuries, there have been examples of men and women whose plans were blessed by God. God commanded Noah to plan and prepare for the flood 120 years in the future. It was his pagan contemporaries who "took no thought for tomorrow" and drowned.

Nehemiah developed a burden for the rebuilding of Jerusalem. He began with prayer and spent four months preparing for an opportunity with the king (Neh. 1). When he finally got his chance to request leave to go to Jerusalem, he was prepared. The king asked how long he would be gone and when he would return.

Immediately, Nehemiah gave him a time (Neh. 2:6). He had done his homework; he figured out how long it would take to get there, get organized, and rebuild the wall. And that's not all; he figured out exactly what he needed in the way of material resources and passports (Neh. 2:7-8). He planned ahead in faith that God would open the door to go. In fact, for Nehemiah, planning was a way of showing God he had faith. Nehemiah shows us that the Holy Spirit can guide just as much in the planning stage as He can in the doing.

The Book of Proverbs is filled with sage advice on planning. "Plan carefully what you do, and whatever you do will turn out right" (4:26, GNB). Solomon refers to the ant who wisely prepares her food in summer for the winter (6:6-8). "Commit your works to the Lord, and your plans will be established" (16:3). "The mind of man plans his way, but the Lord directs his steps" (16:9). Farmers have to plan lest they miss the plowing season and have nothing to harvest (20:4). We are cautioned, "Don't go charging into battle without a plan" (20:18, GNB), and assured, "The plans of the diligent lead surely to advantage, but everyone who is hasty comes surely to poverty" (21:5).

If you study the life of the Apostle Paul, you will discover that he planned his ministry at least a year in advance. Do a study on the word *winter* in his writings. Notice all the things Paul plans to do before winter and after winter. He urges Timothy to visit before winter (2 Tim. 4:21). Why before winter? Because when winter set in, navigation on the Mediterranean was dangerous. If Timothy didn't come before winter, he would have to wait until spring; and Paul's time of departure was close at hand. Before winter or never! Some goals may never be reached unless they are done "before winter."

The Pauline Epistles give frequent glimpses of Paul's plans. In Romans 15, Paul tells of his plans to visit Rome on his way to Spain. In 1 Corinthians 16, he informs the Corinthians of his plans to stay at Ephesus until Pentecost, then go to Macedonia on his way to Corinth. Not all of Paul's plans came to fruition, but without plans, his ministry would have been in shambles. With planning, Paul tried to respond to God's guidance in the most effective way possible.

Planning is not unspiritual—there is no other way to do things "properly and in an orderly manner" (1 Cor. 14:40). The Lord Jesus expects us to plan and prepare: "For which one of you, when he wants to build a tower, does not first sit down and calculate the cost, to see if he has enough to complete it? Otherwise, when he has laid a foundation, and is not able to finish, all who observe it begin to ridicule him, saying, 'This man began to build and was not able to finish' " (Luke 14:28-30). He warns us of the consequences of not preparing in the Parable of the 10 Virgins (Matt. 25:1-13). The 5 wise virgins planned ahead—taking extra oil for their lamps. The 5 foolish virgins took no oil and ran out; they were excluded from the wedding feast.

In the "GAP" method of time management, *planning* is the third stage (after *goals* and *analysis*). "Therefore be careful how you walk, not as unwise men, but as wise" (Eph. 5:15). We may "understand what the will of the Lord is" (Eph. 5:17) and even make His goals our goals, but unless we chart a course, we will never arrive. Being careful how we walk implies knowing where to put the next step. Obstacles will show up along the way and there may be alternative paths to choose from, but we need to start with a plan. We need to plan our itinerary in a way that makes the most of our time.

## A *Sanctified* To-do List

Ivy Lee's method of writing down what I have to do in order of importance and tackling one item at a time has helped me more than any other time-management tool. However, I found one major problem with this technique. My *to-do list* was a reflection of *my* plans—not the Lord's. I had the frustrating experience of seeing very little accomplished. "He thwarts the plans of the crafty, so that their hands achieve no success" (Job 5:12, NIV). I often found out too late I should have been spending my time on something that didn't even make my list. " 'Woe to the obstinate children,' declares the Lord, 'To those who carry out plans that are not Mine' " (Isa. 30:1, NIV). The problem with Ivy Lee's method is that it can involve presumptuous planning—not in accordance with God's will.

The missing ingredient in Lee's method is *prayer!* "If any of you lacks wisdom, let him ask of God, who gives to all men generously and without reproach, and it will be given to him" (James 1:5). "Commit your works to the Lord, and your plans will be established" (Prov. 16:3). "The mind of man plans his way, but the Lord directs his steps" (Prov. 16:9). Prayer makes for a *sanctified to-do list.*

I like to spend five minutes or so in my daily quiet time prayerfully planning the day's activities. I construct a *to-do list* on a three by five card—jotting down everything that comes to mind as I pray. Asking for God's direction seems to open up the flood gates. I am often reminded of several things that would not have made the list had I not prayed.

I also remember to put down anything which was on my mind when I wakened. I often find this is God's way of urging me to do something immediately. "He awakens me morning by morning, He awakens my ear to listen as a disciple" (Isa. 50:4).

One morning, I awakened with the impression that I should pray for a distant friend, only to find out a few days later that he was in desperate trouble at the time. On another occasion, I woke up thinking it was time to check the oil in our car. When I did, the oil level didn't even show on the dip stick!

After putting down everything you can think of, number the items in order of importance. Again, prayer is the key to keeping your priorities straight. (The biblical principles discussed in the chapter on priorities may also help.) Because there may be two or more items of equal priority, it will help to classify under three categories:

    *A*   top priority
    *B*   medium priority
    *C*   lowest priority

Also remember to ask which items can be delegated and which can be put off until tomorrow (usually low-priority items).

Exhibit 9-1 is an example of one of my *to-do lists.* Notice the list is in two parts: *On the job* and *On my own.* This way my priorities at home will not conflict with my priorities at work or vice versa. Each item is given a priority level (A1, A2, and A3).

This gives me an order of attack. A3 is just as important as A1 but it can't be done until later in the day because of scheduling problems. As each item is completed, I cross it off the list. Happiness is a crossed-off *to do list*. "Desire realized is sweet to the soul" (Prov. 13:19).

## Scheduling

We have already seen how the Lord Jesus arranged His ministry by a timetable. We have examined the schedules and deadlines with which Noah, Nehemiah, and Paul planned their ministries.

Scheduling is an important part of 20th-century business. Schedules and deadlines give an urgency to activities that might otherwise drag.

Early in my experience with research and development, I found that identifying a project and assigning a priority to it is not enough. Things don't begin to move until we make a schedule including: (1) the specific tasks to be done, (2) the people responsible, and (3) definite due dates. I have also found that due dates are meaningless unless the person responsible gives his own estimated completion date. Unless all of my staff agree on WHAT should be done, WHO should do it, and WHEN it should be completed, other jobs will take priority and the project will stagnate.

The importance of a timetable suggests a second modification of our *sanctified to-do list*. It is good to estimate the time for doing each task and to schedule it for the most appropriate time during the day (see Exhibits 9-1 and 9-2).

We have already noted that doing the most important item first is not always possible (with all due respect to Ivy Lee). For example, the most important item on my *to-do list* might be a meeting with my staff. I may not be able to schedule it first thing in the morning; it may have to be delayed until afternoon. Further, I must estimate how long the meeting will take before I can schedule it. If it will take all afternoon, and I have an appointment at 3 P.M., it will have to be delayed until tomorrow morning.

Budgeting time is just as important as budgeting finances. In business, time *is* money. A good steward of time will want to treat

## EXHIBIT 9-1  TO-DO LIST

| ACTIVITY * | PRIORITY | ESTIMATED TIME (Hrs.) |
|---|---|---|
| **ON THE JOB** | | |
| R & D staff meeting | A—3 | 1.0 |
| Prepare monthly report | A—1 | 1.5 |
| Prepare seminar | A—2 | 1.5 |
| Write article for journal | C—3 | 15.0 |
| Review patent situation | B—2 | 1.0 |
| UF review meeting | C—1 | 1.0 |
| Review Bob's report | C—2 | 0.75 |
| Take wife to lunch | B—1 | 1.0 |
| **ON MY OWN** | | |
| Neighborhood Bible study | A—1 | 1.5 |
| Prepare sermon outline | B | 1.0 |
| Change oil in car | C—2 | 1.0 |
| Begin sermon research | C—3 | 5.0 |
| Talk with Warner about decision for Christ | A—2 | 0.5 |
| Review math with Tim for quiz | C—1 | 1.0 |

* Notice that routine daily activities do not appear even though high in priority (e.g., quiet time, jogging, opening mail).

**EXHIBIT 9-2** SCHEDULE* FOR WEDNESDAY AND THURSDAY
(Using *TO-DO LIST* of Exhibit 9-1)

| | February 24 | February 25 |
|---|---|---|
| 8:00 | Prepare monthly report | Review patent situation |
| 8:30 | | |
| 9:00 | | |
| 9:30 | | |
| 10:00 | | UF review meeting |
| 10:30 | Prepare seminar | |
| 11:00 | | |
| 11:30 | | |
| 12:00 | Take wife to lunch | |
| 12:30 | | |
| 1:00 | | Read Bob's report |
| 1:30 | | |
| 2:00 | | |
| 2:30 | Prepare for R & D staff mtg. | |
| 3:00 | R & D staff meeting | Begin to write article |
| 3:30 | | for journal |
| 4:00 | | |
| 4:30 | | |
| 5:00 | | |
| 5:30 | | Change oil in car |
| 6:00 | | |
| 6:30 | | |
| 7:00 | | |
| 7:30 | Neighborhood Bible study | Review math with Tim |
| 8:00 | | |
| 8:30. | | |
| 9:00 | Talk with Warner about Christ | Begin sermon research |
| 9:30 | | |
| 10:00 | Prepare sermon outline | |
| 10:30 | | |
| 11:00 | | |

*To see how the schedule actually materialized, see Exhibits 6-1 through 6-3 (time inventory of these two days).

it with the same respect that he treats his money. In a financial budget we are either told how much money is available to do a job, or we are asked how much it will take. Likewise, with a time budget, we need to estimate how long it will take to complete a project. More commonly, we are given a deadline and must do the best we can with the time available. Advertising agencies start with the date they want the ad to appear and then work backward to determine due dates for concept, rough copy, layouts, photography, and art boards. Large wall calendars are helpful in scheduling. (Personally, I like to keep all deadlines and appointments in a pocket calendar.)

This type of scheduling is not limited to big business. The student who is given several books to read by a certain time figures out how many pages he has to read each day and in what order. The Sunday School teacher given 13 weeks in the quarter, figures out what subjects to cover, how much time he should spend on each, and in what sequence. The housewife finds out her husband's boss is coming home for dinner. She figures out how long each course will take to prepare and when to start so each will be ready at the right time. I believe Teddy Roosevelt knew what he was talking about when he said, "Nine-tenths of wisdom consists in being wise in scheduling time." I also believe *that* wisdom is available from God (James 1:5).

The most difficult part of scheduling is estimating the time required for each item. Ivy Lee seemed unconcerned about this, but without a self-imposed deadline, a 30-minute task can become an all-day project. According to Parkinson's Law; "Work expands so as to fill the time available." Giving ourselves a deadline can help us complete the job in a reasonable amount of time.

Self-imposed deadlines keep us on our overall schedule. If my wife gives herself 20 minutes to clean the bathroom, she knows she can clean the sink and toilet, hang fresh towels, gather dirty clothes, and throw away soap wrappers. But she also knows this is not the day to recaulk around the tub or scrub the tiles. Twenty minutes is all the time she has allotted.

Where did she come up with 20 minutes? Past experience. Her time inventory tells her how long it usually takes to clean the bathroom, prepare a meal, or vacuum the house. Armed with this information, she can allocate time according to a schedule.

A pocket timer makes this a fun game. Set it for 20 minutes and see if you can beat your previous record. I find this gimmick especially good for enforced skimming of certain magazines. I give myself no more than 15 minutes. When the buzzer goes off, I toss out the magazine and move on to the next one.

Someone may be worried that self-imposed deadlines encourage sloppiness—that quality is sacrificed for time. The 80/20 rule reassures us.

## The 80/20 Rule

If you understand the *80/20 rule*, you can probably spend up to 80 percent less time on a given project without sacrificing more than 20 percent of the benefits.

The *80/20 rule* is sometimes known as the *Pareto time principle* after the 19th-century Italian economist and sociologist Velfredo Pareto (Figure 4). He discovered that 20 percent of the people in Italy controlled 80 percent of the wealth. He noticed that the truly significant items in any group normally constitute a relatively small portion of the total number of items in the group. His principle is sometimes referred to as the concept of the *vital few* or the *trivial many*.

It's uncanny how universal his principle is:

80% of the sales volume is generated from 20% of the product line.

80% of the sales come from 20% of the customers.

80% of a product's cost is concentrated in 20% of the components.

80% of the total sick leave is taken by 20% of the employees.

80% of your washing is done on 20% of your wardrobe.

80% of a pastor's time is spent with 20% of his people.

80% of the giving comes from 20% of the members.

80% of the relevant information can be transmitted with 20% of the words.

In the area of time management, the *80/20 rule* may be stated as follows: "Eighty percent of the value is gained during the first

# PARETO TIME PRINCIPLE (80/20 RULE)

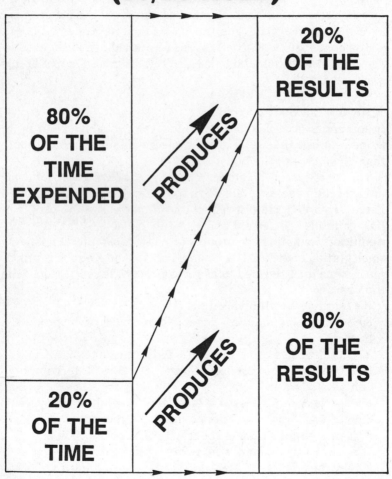

Figure 4

20 percent of our work." For example, if I spend 20 hours preparing a sermon, the first 4 hours will produce 80 percent of the value delivered in that sermon. The other 16 hours will simply polish and perfect it.

Since most of us can't get everything done that needs to get done, the *80/20 rule* gives some helpful insight into this problem:

- Shortening the time spent on any task may not appreciably diminish the return.
- Setting a self-imposed deadline for completing the task may help avoid the non-productive final phase.
- The perfectionist always encounters the law of diminishing returns.
- Many activities in our lives can be dropped without diminishing our overall effectiveness.

I believe the Lord Jesus, perfect as He was, saw the realities of the *80/20 rule*. He left many unhealed and many untaught, but He completed His mission on schedule. All of us can think of more He could have done, but none of us would dare suggest that His three-and-a-half-year ministry was anything less than God's perfect plan.

How can we apply the *80/20 rule*? Projects we do repetitively are usually the best places to start. Picking up after children, preparing for a Sunday School lesson, correspondence with friends are examples. Can we spend less time with substantially the same results? Remember, we don't want to sacrifice quality; we only want to stop short of gilding the lily.

Another caution: Apply the *80/20 rule* to individual projects or tasks, but never to a complete schedule. Scheduling one event after the other with too little time for each is like rigging a sailboat too tightly. There needs to be enough slack for the sails to give with the wind; otherwise they tear themselves to pieces trying to resist. We need to schedule breathing space into our days, or our bodies and minds can give out like the too-taut sails. A good rule of thumb is to schedule 50 percent more time than we think we need for each task. It's satisfying to beat the schedule and we can always fill the spaces.

## A Time for Everything

Solomon said, "There is a time for everything, and a reason for every activity under heaven:

a time to plant and a time to uproot,
a time to tear down and a time to build,
a time to keep and a time to throw away,"
(Ecc. 3:1-3, 6, NIV).

The scheduling of activities in the most effective order is not always as surefire as Ivy Lee suggests. Even though the project has top priority, the coming together of other events and inputs may dictate putting it off until tomorrow. Tackling the project *now* may be a waste of time.

Making a scheduling decision before all the facts are in may be the height of folly. Putting God first may not always mean having a quiet time at 6 A.M. It may be impossible for a nursing mother.

The best time for an activity will depend not only on external circumstances, but also on internal metabolism. Each person has a fairly predictable daily pattern when energy is highest, concentration is best, drowsiness is likely, and irritability is possible. Some people are more irritable before meals when their blood sugar is low.

Research shows that the best time of the day for most people to memorize is between 8 A.M. and 10 A.M. The nervous system is assimilating fewer new impressions at those early hours. The ability to remember drops 10 percent later in the day (D. V. Lewis, *How to Build Memory Skills*, Education for Management, Inc., p. 15).

To optimize your schedule ask, "When do I study best? When do I have the most energy? Am I drowsy in the afternoon? When am I most congenial? When should I stay away from people?" Identify your internal prime time (the time when you do your clearest thinking) and your external prime time (when you are best with others). Then try to match your activities with your biorhythms. Reserve your internal prime time for those activities which require greatest concentration. This is why item A-1 comes earlier in the day than A-2 on the *to-do list* of Exhibit 9-1 and the schedule of Exhibit 9-2.

The most scientific way to detect your metabolic peaks is to keep an accurate hourly record of your temperature for a couple of days. Peak efficiency will be reached when your temperature is higher than the normal average. Do your toughest assignments at those times.

Whether you are a morning or a night person is also a factor. Morning people recover rapidly from sleep; they wake up early raring to go. They get a lot done before lunch. But by 4 P.M. they might as well go home; they're dragging. By contrast, night people have a hard time waking up; they don't function until 11 A.M., but by 5 P.M. they're going strong and can often work until midnight and beyond. Neither type is abnormal; their biological clocks differ by 6 to 12 hours. Learn your own biorhythm and plan your toughest work for prime times.

With all due respect to night people, most high achievers tend to be early risers. For example, Charles Gimble, the great merchandiser, when asked how he accomplished so much, replied, "I have lived three years longer than the average person; I get up early!" Even in the first century, Pliny the Elder wrote, "The human race owes all of its achievements to the rooster—because it rouses men from slumber." In our own day, the one thing common to most success stories is the alarm clock. "How long wilt thou sleep, O sluggard? When wilt thou arise out of thy sleep? Yet a little sleep, a little slumber, a little folding of the hands to sleep (Prov. 6:9-10, KJV).

Perhaps this is not really a bias toward morning people but against those who linger in the sack. You may think you need a full 8 hours of sleep every night. But have you ever thought of applying the *80/20 rule* to your sleep schedule? Sometimes the 8-hour pattern is a habit and can be reduced without endangering your health or reducing your efficiency. According to sleep expert Dr. Robert van De Castle, you can thrive on less sleep. He suggests reducing the amount of sleep you get bit by bit. For instance, try waking up just 10 minutes earlier for a few days. Then extend it to 15 or 20 minutes. Within a month you should be able to shorten your overall sleeping time by an hour-and-a-half. Reducing your sleep time by even 1 hour a night can give you

23 extra 16-hour days every year. Dr. van De Castle says you'll know when you've gone too far, because you'll find yourself tired and nervous.

Once you've established a good sleep schedule, don't change the pattern on weekends. It will be harder to get back in the groove on Sunday night.

If you have trouble sleeping, it sometimes helps to get up and pray. Or, if you're worrying about a problem, grab a piece of paper and start outlining possible solutions. Then commit them to the Lord and return to bed.

For me, prime time is often early in the morning before anybody else is awake. There are no distractions, no phone calls, and quiet reigns. I like to reserve most of that time for meeting with the Lord.

If you don't have a good feel for when you're at your best, try keeping a record for a week, classifying each hour of the day as follows:

P for prime time when you are sharpest and at peak efficiency

A for average capability

D for when you're dragging (fatigued and slow mentally)

O for obnoxious with others

Planning may make the difference between success or failure in your life. I'm convinced you can increase your own effectiveness by over 50 percent if you use a *sanctified to-do list*—praying about *what* God wants you to do, *when* He wants you to do it, and giving yourself a deadline for completion. For still greater increases, apply the 80/20 rule and prime-time concepts.

Try it, and let me know what you think it is worth.

# 10

# Procrastination: Good or Bad?

After I became a Christian, I began to think of all my high school buddies who were missing the boat. I wrote letters to some, sharing my new-found faith in Christ. I figured I would see others at Christmas or by summer at the latest.

James was particularly on my heart. He was a year ahead of me and had gone to the University of Chicago. We had become close friends because of a common interest in astronomy. Some people thought he was a genius, and I think his IQ was in that bracket. I planned to see him during the summer.

Summer came, but I didn't see James very much. When we did get together, I was so awed by what he was doing in physics at the University of Chicago, talking about religion seemed out of place.

Other summers came and went. James sure had a lot going for him; he seemed so self-sufficient. I still wanted to share with him when the time was ripe.

As the years went by, I saw less and less of James. He went to the University of Louisville to get his doctorate in physics. Louisville was home for both of us, but our paths didn't cross that much. One Christmas (1962), I was determined not to delay any longer. I purposed to share Christ and query James on his spiritual condition. We saw each other, but we were never alone. Somehow it just didn't work out. "Oh well, there will be other times," I told myself.

One night in the spring of 1963, I received a long-distance phone call from Louisville. James had committed suicide the night before. He had gone into his laboratory late that Sunday night, tied a plastic bag over his head, and lain down to die. I couldn't believe it. He had so much going for him; he was a genius! He was about to receive his doctorate; what a waste.

A day or two later, a letter from him arrived. It was a poem in German, expressing the despair of a man without Christ. I cried a long time that night. His blood was on my hands. How terrible is procrastination!

I also mourn for the procrastination of others. Friends who have been urged to get right with God and have put it off; friends who have better things to do, accumulating wealth, eating, drinking, and having fun. "Maybe someday," they say. But the day comes when God says, "Fool! This night your soul is required of you; and the things you have prepared, whose will they be?" (Luke 12:20, RSV)

## Come before Winter

When Paul sensed the time of his departure was at hand, he wrote to Timothy, "Make every effort to come before winter" (2 Tim. 4:21). Don't procrastinate Timothy; before winter or never! There are some opportunities which will be lost forever unless they are seized "before winter." One meaning of the phrase "redeeming the time" is to seize opportunity before it is lost.

Suppose that Timothy, when he received Paul's letter, had said to himself, "Yes, I must go to Rome; but first of all I must clear up some matters here at Ephesus." Eventually the matters are resolved, and Timothy sets out for Troas to get a ship for Rome. He is told that the season for navigation is over, "No ships for Italy until April!" When April finally comes, Timothy sails on the first ship for Rome. Upon arrival he seeks out Paul's prison only to be told, "Don't you know, Paul was beheaded last month? Wait a minute, he left a message for you, 'Give my love to Timothy, when he comes, if he comes.' "

"Come before winter." There are favorable seasons. I can re- member as a young Christian struggling with a besetting sin. One night, sitting at my desk, I was assailed by the enemy and was about to yield. Suddenly, it was as if the Lord stood before me saying, "This is your hour. If you yield to this temptation now, it will destroy you. If you conquer it now, you are its master forev- er." I obeyed, refused the tempter, and emerged victorious. To many a person there comes an hour when destiny knocks—a turning point in the history of his soul. This is the hour of opportu- nity in which the chains of evil habit can be broken. If we do not seize opportunity, they will bind us forever. "Behold, now is the accepted time; behold, now is the day of salvation" (2 Cor. 6:2, KJV).

The Battle of Gettysburg was the turning point in the Civil War. The Union Army had been driven from its position on Seminary Ridge and was retreating in considerable disorder. The Yankee hope was for a break in the Confederate assault so they could regroup on nearby Cemetery Ridge in a strong defensive position. But there were still four hours of daylight, plenty of time for the Southerners to rout the Northern Army then and there.

Lieutenant General Richard S. Ewell, the Confederate com- mander in charge, had three whole divisions under him, two of which were fresh. Had he turned those divisions loose on the Union Army that afternoon, we might be a divided nation today.

General Ewell sat on the ground under an apple tree that after- noon mulling over the situation. Unable to make up his mind whether to pursue or not to pursue, he decided to wait until morning. This allowed the Union Army to regroup.

The next day (July 2), the Confederates failed in assaults on Cemetery Ridge. On July 3rd, Lee sent Longstreet with G. E. Pickett's division in their famous charge against the Union center, but the Union Army was too well entrenched; Longstreet was beaten back. On July 4th, Lee withdrew in defeat. Ewell's golden opportunity passed forever.

Shakespeare wrote, "There is a tide in the affairs of men, which, taken at the flood, leads on to fortune; omitted, all the voyage of their life is bound in shallows and in miseries; and we must take the current when it serves, or lose our ventures" (*Julius Caesar*, Act IV, Scene 3).

Procrastination plagues all of us. More plans go astray, more dreams go unfulfilled, and more time is wasted by procrastination than by any other cause. For many people the thing that ruins their careers, destroys their happiness, and even shortens their lives is procrastination. An old tombstone reads:

> He walked beneath the moon
> and slept beneath the sun.
> He lived a life of going to do
> and died with nothing done.

The word *procrastinate* in the Latin comes from *pro* which means forward and *cras* which means tomorrow. Hence, to procrastinate is to put forward until tomorrow. For example, it is postponing activities with our children because we have more urgent things to do. Then one day the children are grown and it's too late to do all the things we talked about doing.

## First Things First

Procrastination can be good if we put off unimportant things or projects which can benefit from the delay. Unfortunately most people would rather put off the important things. We too often substitute activities of lower priority.

> I've gone for a drink and sharpened my pencils,
> Searched through my desk for forgotten utensils,
> Reset my watch and adjusted my chair,
> Loosened my tie and straightened my hair,
> Filled my pen and tested the blotter,
> Gone for another drink of water,
> Adjusted the calendar, raised the blinds,
> Sorted erasers of different kinds.
> Now, down to work I can finally sit
> Oops! Too late, it's time to quit!
>
> Leonard A. Paris

Busy-work activities are deceptive; they provide a feeling of activity and accomplishment. A lot of people justify putting important things off to the last minute by claiming they work better under the pressure of a deadline. I find myself doing it subconsciously. The trouble is we don't work better; we only work faster. Granted, the 80/20 rule helps us squeak by, but it's unfair to others working on the same project who are waiting for our input. And there are other problems with this approach: the copy machine often breaks down at the last moment or the secretary is out sick.

Putting off an A-1 activity can be costly. If we delay servicing our cars, we may have expensive breakdowns on our hands. If we delay going to the dentist, we may have to live with false teeth.

Further, as long as an important task remains undone, it weighs us down psychologically. Each time we think of it, we become more demoralized; worrying about it undermines our work on other tasks.

The psychological lift of accomplishment will enable us to sail through other projects with the greatest of ease. Procrastination is like the law of inertia. It's more difficult to get moving than to stay moving.

## Why Do We Procrastinate?

Understanding why we procrastinate is half the battle in overcoming it. There are three major causes: either the task is unpleasant, difficult, or requires tough decisions.

*Unpleasant Tasks.* For most people, this is the greatest single cause of procrastination. We postpone an unpleasant task, attempting to make life easier for ourselves. Ironically, putting off a task only increases the unpleasantness, since the task will seldom disappear.

The sluggard of Proverbs postpones work because it is unpleasant to him. When we ask him "How long?" or "When?" he does not refuse us, but pleads for a delay: "Yet a little sleep, a little slumber, a little folding of the hands to sleep" (Prov. 6:9-10, KJV). "The sluggard will not plow by reason of the cold; therefore shall he beg in harvest, and have nothing" (Prov. 20:4, KJV). Even though the product of his labor is essential to survival, he avoids the task because it is too cold.

"The slothful man roasteth not that which he took in hunting" (Prov. 12:27, KJV), because he enjoys hunting more than cleaning and cooking. That is too dirty—too unpleasant for him.

Sometimes the sluggard is afraid of imagined unpleasantness. "The slothful man saith, 'There is a lion in the way; a lion is in the streets' " (Prov. 26:13, KJV). Likewise we avoid unpleasant tasks (like firing a long-term employee, going to the dentist, or meeting with an obnoxious client) because we're afraid. However, more often than not, the unpleasantness fails to materialize.

Sometimes we procrastinate because we're afraid of failure, and that's unpleasant. In the Parable of the Talents, the unprofitable servant buried his talent because he was afraid he would lose it (Matt. 25:24-30).

*Difficult Tasks.* Oddly enough, we also tend to postpone enjoyable tasks as well as those we abhor. Usually, it's because the task is overwhelming; it seems to be more than we can handle. A student may thoroughly enjoy a certain course, but he puts off studying for the big test. I enjoy writing, but the idea of writing a whole book is overwhelming, and I tend to procrastinate. Ironically, knowing that a difficult task looms over us tires us out more than working on the task itself. "Nothing is so fatiguing," said William James, "as the eternal hanging on of an uncompleted task."

For this reason, given two projects of equal priority, it is always better to begin with the more difficult one. It's better to attack it while we're fresh and enthusiastic. Less difficult tasks can be done later, even though we're not at peak efficiency.

It was the difficulty of the task that stopped Moses from responding to God's call to lead the Israelites out of Egypt (Ex. 3—4). He argued with God and procrastinated.

*Indecision* is the third major cause of procrastination. It usually stems from a strong desire to be right, to avoid being wrong, or a desire for perfection. Take an investment decision. The sum of money at risk is substantial, and I can't afford to be wrong. The investment itself is not unpleasant or even difficult, but I need to make a wise decision. I procrastinate, leaning one direction and then the other. If the decision is delayed too long, the opportunity will pass, and the decision will be made for me.

Your *time inventory* can help you discover *why* you procrastinate. You may be able to spot diversionary activities that didn't really need to be done. You probably did them to avoid working on a specific assignment. Was it unpleasant or too difficult? Or were you avoiding a decision? Look also for simple activities that took more time than they should; you were probably stalling to avoid the big one. Now take some time to analyze your procrastination habits and ask yourself the following questions:

- What do I tend to put off, or delay, most often?
- What am I currently putting off?
- How do I know when I'm procrastinating? Do I have a set of favorite replacement activities?
- What happens when I procrastinate? Are the results positive or negative?
- What causes my procrastination? (Try to link a specific cause to each task you put off.)

## Putting off Procrastination

What can be done to get out of the rut of procrastination? The remedy will depend on why you procrastinate: unpleasant tasks, difficult tasks, or indecision.

*Unpleasant Tasks.* If this is a cause, count the cost of delay and ask what problems you are likely to create for yourself. Concentrate on the benefits inherent in completing the task. A homemaker may despise housework, but if she enjoys a clean house she will do it. Making a list of benefits derived from completing the task often motivates us to get started and follow through.

The Lord Jesus motivated His disciples to risk suffering and even death because of rewards in the life to come. "Do not fear what you are about to suffer. . . . Be faithful until death, and I will give you the crown of life" (Rev. 2:10).

Break down the unpleasant task into small pieces. We can endure anything for a few minutes. We may find it's not so unpleasant after all, once we get moving. Some of the mini-tasks may actually be fun. For example, if we've been putting off washing the 20 windows in our houses, we can try washing 1 window each day.

Let as many other people know about your project as possible. You can tell the barber, pastor, boss, and secretary about it. Every time you see them, they will generally ask about your project—just to make small talk. This is motivational, because it's painful and embarrassing to admit you still haven't done it—even more unpleasant than the task itself.

Promise yourself a reward for completing the task. Ernest Hemingway kept careful track of his daily output as a writer and rewarded himself with pleasurable activities in direct proportion to that output. Think about what leisure and fun activities you can reward yourself with. Perhaps you would like to take yourself to lunch or a night out at the movies. Give yourself Friday afternoon off for finishing the unpleasant project by noon. Or give yourself a weekend vacation after you finish painting the house.

Find someone to do the unpleasant task with you. The task will be finished sooner and you will enjoy the fellowship. You may even be able to use it in discipling your partner.

Hire someone else to do it. Sometimes the cost of hiring someone to paint the house makes good sense psychologically.

*Difficult Tasks.* Often we avoid difficult tasks because we simply don't know where to start. The task may be so complex that it overwhelms us. We need to find some way to reduce the apparent complexity so the task no longer appears difficult. Breaking the overwhelming task into smaller subtasks is a great help; this was Nehemiah's approach to rebuilding the wall of Jerusalem. The only way he could do it in 52 days was to break this overwhelming project into manageable parts (Neh. 3). We can start doing the easier parts first—building up momentum for the more difficult ones. We may even be able to delegate some of the smaller tasks. As each subtask is completed, there is a sense of accomplishment that drives us on to completion. I believe this is why the Lord has chosen not to reveal His entire blueprint for our lives. If He did, we would probably expire on the spot. Instead, He reveals it one step at a time.

The second idea is what Alan Lakein calls "the Swiss cheese method." In *How to Get Control of Your Time and Your Life*, he says the way to overwhelm overwhelming tasks is to poke some holes in them. He calls these holes *instant tasks*. An *instant task* requires five minutes or less and makes some sort of hole in your overwhelming A-1. For example, each of the following is an *instant task;* pulling together relevant paper work, deciding on the people you'll need to contact, arranging a meeting to discuss it, making a list of the various subtasks involved, making a schedule for completing each of the subtasks. Once you've started working on the *instant task*, you're much more likely to keep working past the five minute deadline. The resulting momentum and immersion will get you interested and absorbed in what you're doing. Further, even if you don't continue past the deadline, the work you accomplish in five minutes will act as a magnet to draw you back to the remainder of the project (Signet, pp. 100-108).

Letting other people know about it also helps with difficult tasks, such as trying to quit smoking or to lose weight.

*Indecision.* There is a time to deliberate and a time to act. The time to decide is when further information will add very little to the quality of the decision. Delay beyond that point seldom improves the decision. No one is always right. The worst course is making no decision or delaying until the opportunity has passed.

We need to make a sincere effort to obtain the best information possible, ask for God's wisdom, make the decision, and move on. "Commit thy way unto the Lord; trust also in Him; and He shall bring it to pass" (Ps. 37:5, KJV). Above all, don't keep fretting and fussing over the decision. Don't keep rehashing it; that's not faith!

Perfectionism is often at the heart of indecision. Budding authors who keep rewriting chapter one, striving for the perfect phrase, seldom publish books. When you are tempted to reach for perfection, recall the 80/20 rule. Eighty percent of the value of the decision-making process comes from the first 20 percent of the effort.

Indecisiveness can often be traced to worries and fears that something will go wrong. Write down all the obstacles and problems; then think of ways they can be solved. Make your decision and commit it to the Lord with thanksgiving. "Be anxious for nothing, but in everything by prayer and supplication with thanksgiving let your requests be made known to God. And the peace of God, which surpasses all comprehension, shall guard your hearts and your minds in Christ Jesus" (Phil. 4:6-7). Do everything you can to develop a do-it-now habit.

## Is Procrastination Always Bad?

Benjamin Franklin was the one who said, "Never put off till tomorrow that which you can do today." But Aaron Burr said, "Never do today what you can put off till tomorrow. Delay may give clearer light as to what is best to be done." Who is right? Both are.

We have already seen why some high-priority tasks are better delayed because of additional input or scheduling considerations such as "prime time."

Low priority items (C tasks) are often put off until tomorrow by default. We can benefit from this 24 hour delay. Perhaps we discover that a low-priority item doesn't need to be done at all. Or our subconscious mind works on it and comes up with a better approach. For this reason, some time-management experts say, "Do nothing today which can just as well be postponed until tomorrow."

When scheduling, you should always ask, "Would this situation benefit from delay?" Many do. Mopping the kitchen floor on a rainy day before the children come home is a waste of time.

Napoleon instructed his secretary, Bourrienne, to leave all his letters unopened for three weeks. He then observed, with great satisfaction, how large a part of the correspondence took care of itself, no longer requiring an answer.

Herman Krannert, management consultant, says, "I sometimes like to measure a man by the things he decides to leave *undone*. The man who insists on getting 100 percent of his job done either doesn't have enough to do or he doesn't have the kind of stuff it takes to succeed in business today." There is such a thing as "creative procrastination."

In John 11, we read that the Lord Jesus deliberately delayed when He heard that Lazarus was sick. For Mary and Martha, His procrastination seemed tragic. "Lord, if you had been here, my brother would not have died" (vv. 21, 32). In the wisdom of Jesus, the delay was designed to bring glory to God. "I am glad for your sakes that I was not there, so that you may believe.... If you believe, you will see the glory of God.... Many therefore of the Jews, who had come to Mary and beheld what He had done, believed in Him" (vv. 15, 40, 45).

The Lord Jesus had a sense of timing which mystified His disciples and brothers. When His brothers were pushing Him to go to the Feast of Tabernacles to perform miracles and display Himself to the world, He said, "My time is not yet at hand, but your time is always opportune" (John 7:6). We are always seeking to push ahead now; but for Jesus, waiting for the right time was more important.

## Wait for God's Timing

Again and again the psalmist urges, "Wait thou on God," yet few Christians are willing to wait for the Lord's timing.

We are like Saul. He was instructed to wait seven days for Samuel to offer burnt offerings and sacrifice peace offerings. The Philistines were assembling to fight Israel; the Israelites began to hide in caves and flee. Samuel was nowhere in sight, so Saul offered the burnt offering himself. At that moment Samuel appeared, demanding: "What have you done? . . . You have acted foolishly; you have not kept the commandment of the Lord your God, . . . now your kingdom shall not endure . . . because you have not kept what the Lord commanded you" (1. Sam. 13:11, 13-14). Saul lost his kingdom because he was not willing to wait for God.

The third stage of the GAP method of time management (planning) is summarized in Ephesians 5:15, "Therefore be careful how you walk, not as unwise men, but as wise." Walking wisely is walking with the Lord. It is walking in the right direction (goals the same as God's), walking at the right pace (not falling behind or getting ahead).

The Lord says, "I will instruct you and teach you in the way which you should go; I will counsel you with My eye upon you. Do not be as the horse or as the mule which have no understanding, whose trappings include bit and bridle to hold them in check, otherwise they will not come near to you" (Ps. 32:8-9). Whereas a stubborn mule will seldom go when you want him to, you can't get a horse to stop when he's headed for home. Horses and mules have no understanding. Our job is to "understand what the will of the Lord is" and then "walk wisely" (Eph. 5:15-17). There are times when we are as stubborn as mules; our procrastination is sin. There are other times when we are as wild as horses—running ahead of the Lord and not waiting for Him. Both can be equally bad. We need to keep in step with God.

# 11

# The Discipline
# of Concentration

The clothes dryer had been on the blink for three weeks. Knowing how busy I was, my wife assured me it was not urgent; she could use the neighbor's until I had time to fix it. I had put it on my *to-do list* promptly, but it was rated C and delayed from day to day for too long. My wife had been very patient; she knew it was on my *to do list*, though I'm sure she would have preferred giving it a higher priority. I moved it to the top of my list (*A-1*) for Saturday and scheduled the whole morning for the job.

First thing Saturday morning I tore into the dryer. After removing the back, I was uncertain how to proceed, so I decided to get the instruction manual which was filed upstairs. When I got to the file cabinet, I noticed a stack of materials to be filed. Disgusted with myself for procrastinating with the dryer, I couldn't bear putting off filing too. Filing the stack would only take 30 minutes to an hour.

While filing, I noticed a letter that had slipped into the stack. It should have been answered three months ago. I decided to do it right then. My friend had asked if he could borrow a pamphlet I had, so I went off to find the pamphlet.

After several minutes of fumbling in a dark closet, I decided to get the flashlight. The batteries were dead, so I put *batteries* on my wife's grocery list and began to look for another flashlight.

While in the kitchen I noticed the faucet was dripping, so I got my tools to change the washer. I shut off the valves under the sink and replaced the washer. I managed at the same time to cut my finger, so I went to the bathroom for a Band-Aid. It was the last one. I bandaged my finger and went back to the kitchen to add *Band-Aids* to my wife's grocery list.

I was just trying to remember why I had come to the kitchen in the first place, when my wife asked if I was hungry. It was lunchtime! "By the way," she asked, "did you get the dryer fixed?"

## Breaking the Rabbit Habit

People who jump at any task that comes along are known as *rabbit chasers*. They are the very opposite of procrastinators. They have no trouble starting a task on their *to-do list*; their trouble is sticking to it.

We can never hope to finish anything until we break the rabbit habit. It will wear us out and we'll have nothing to show for it.

D. L. Moody said, "Give me a man who says, 'This one thing I do' like Paul and not, 'These 50 things I dabble in.' " Moody was referring to Philippians 3:12-14, "I press on to take hold of that for which Christ Jesus took hold of me. Brothers, I do not consider myself yet to have taken hold of it. *But one thing I do:* forgetting what is behind and straining toward what is ahead, I press on toward the goal to win the prize for which God has called me heavenward in Christ Jesus" (NIV). The Apostle Paul concentrated on one goal at a time. He often used the spectacle of the footrace (popular in the athletic games of the Roman empire) as a figure for the Christian life. In Hebrews 12:1-2 we read, "Therefore, since we have so great a cloud of witnesses surrounding us, let us also lay aside every encumbrance, and the sin which so easily entangles us, and let us run with endurance the race that is set before us, fixing our eyes on Jesus, the author and perfecter of faith, who for the joy set before Him endured the cross, despising the shame, and has sat down at the right hand of the throne of God."

Again in 1 Corinthians 9:24-27, "Do you not know that in a race all the runners run, but only one gets the prize? Run in such a way as to get the prize. Everyone who competes in the games goes into strict training. They do it to get a crown that will not last; but we do it to get a crown that will last forever. Therefore I do not run like a man running aimlessly; I do not fight like a man beating the air. No, I beat my body and make it my slave so that after I have preached to others, I myself will not be disqualified for the prize" (NIV).

Notice how Paul focuses on the prize: "Straining toward what is ahead, I press on toward the goal to win the prize." "Let us run with endurance the race that is set before us, fixing our eyes on Jesus." "Run in such a way as to get the prize. . . . I do not run like a man running aimlessly." We are to know our goals and not be diverted from them. We are to spend all our energies to win the prize at the finish.

John Baker surprised everyone by winning his first cross-country race, defeating the state champion, and setting a new record. How? He focused on only one goal at a time—to pass the runner in front of him. Once that goal was accomplished, he set a new goal of passing the next runner, and then the next. He concentrated on one at a time.

The successful runner has a single eye—with undivided attention on the goal at hand. In his book *A Strategy for Daily Living*, Dr. Ari Kiev, of the Cornell Medical Center writes, "Observing the lives of people who have mastered adversity, I have repeatedly noted that they have established goals and, irrespective of obstacles, have sought with all their effort to achieve them. From the moment they've fixed an objective in their minds and decided to concentrate all their energies on a specific goal, they began to surmount the most difficult odds" (Free Press, p. 3).

Men and women greatly used of God have sensed the high calling of God and have refused to be distracted from that calling. Billy Graham became the world's leading evangelist because he concentrated on evangelism, refusing opportunities to get involved in Christian education or national politics. He focuses on what God called him to do and moves toward that goal with determination.

In the Hebrews 12 passage, we are told to fix our eyes on Jesus "the forerunner and finisher of our faith." Jesus fixed His eyes on *one* goal at a time. Luke records, "When the days were approaching for His ascension, He resolutely set His face to go to Jerusalem" (9:51). Even though the Pharisees warned that Herod wanted to kill Him, He was determined: "Nevertheless, I must journey on today and tomorrow and the next day; for it cannot be that a prophet should perish outside of Jerusalem ... the third day I reach My goal" (13:33, 32). When Peter objected, He replied, "Get behind Me, Satan! You are a stumbling block to Me; for you are not setting your mind on God's interests, but man's" (Matt. 16:23).

Instead of focusing on one goal at a time as Jesus did, we often try to go in all directions at once. It is as though we are trying to take on the attributes of God—omnipresence and omnipotence in particular. Jesus as God incarnate voluntarily gave up His right to omnipresence, showing us how to concentrate on one thing at a time. "Who though He existed in the form of God, did not regard equality with God a thing to be grasped, but emptied Himself, taking the form of a bond-servant, and being made in the likeness of men. And being found in appearance as a man, He humbled Himself by becoming obedient to the point of death, even death on a cross" (Phil. 2:6-8). Following Him does not mean doing everything at once. He didn't.

There are three hindrances which prevent us from concentrating on our goals: diversionary activities, debilitating recollections, and entangling sins.

## Diversionary Activities

When Paul wrote, "One thing I do ... I press on toward *the* goal" (Phil. 3:13-14) he implied that there are diversionary activities— other things which keep us from our number one priority. These other activities can be harmless and legitimate in and of themselves, but they distract us from our primary goal. For example, "No soldier in active service entangles himself in the affairs of everyday life so that he may please the one who enlists him as a soldier" (2 Tim. 2:4).

Further, the peace and calmness we admire in the life of Jesus did not come from an attitude of hurry-hurry, but from a life that concentrated on one goal at a time. Jesus knew when to say *no* to diversionary activities. When He sent out the 70, His instructions were to "greet no one on the way" and "do not keep moving from house to house" (Luke 10:4, 7). This was not because He was antisocial, but because these activities would divert from His goal.

When Elisha sent Gehazi, his servant, to raise up the Shunammite's son, his instructions were: "Gird up your loins . . . and go your way; if you meet any man, do not salute him, and if anyone salutes you, do not answer him" (2 Kings 4:29). There was no time for socializing when a boy lay dead.

Likewise, Nehemiah achieved His goal because he knew how to say *no* to diversionary activities: "I am doing a great work and I cannot come down. Why should the work stop while I leave it and come down to you?" (Neh. 6:3)

Most of our diversionary activities are not interruptions over which we have no control, but ones we choose. This was vividly demonstrated to me one day at the office. I had a little accident; I bent over and heard a rip! To my accute embarrassment, I had ripped the seam in the seat of my pants. Instead of trotting all over the building as usual, I stayed unusually close to my desk. I used the phone a lot. I called meetings in my office. I even asked the president to step in when he next went by. I discovered at the end of the day that I had accomplished more work than I usually did in a week. I wasted no time in friendly chitchat, and of course, I stayed until everybody else had gone home, accomplishing even more. By staying at my desk, I had been able to concentrate on the tasks at hand.

We often pursue diversionary activities fearing we will forget them unless we handle them immediately. A three by five index card comes to the rescue here. Simply jot down the task that comes to mind; it may be a worthy candidate for tomorrow's *to-do list* but should not be allowed to distract us from today's tasks. Jotting it down frees us from worry that we will forget it.

Further, don't try to mix work and play. One of the best pieces of advice I received from my freshman advisor at M.I.T. was, "When you work, work hard. When you play, play hard." Later when I became a Christian, I found Colossians 3:23 contained the same idea, "And whatsoever ye do, do it heartily" (KJV). Taking work along on a vacation will only undermine our rejuvenation.

There is, of course, some justification for taking a break from concentrated work. "Much study is a weariness of the flesh" (Ecc. 12:12, RSV). However, most of us take too many breaks. In general, 20 periods of 10 minutes each are not as effective as one sustained period of 60 minutes. The ability to persevere, without distraction on the same task for long periods of time will pay handsome rewards. Men with the self-discipline to do this, though average in intelligence, have achieved more than geniuses.

The sole exception to doing only one thing at a time is *eyes-and-hands-work* (discussed in chapter 8). It's an exception because this type of activity requires no concentration. Therefore we can double up with another activity requiring total concentration. Eyes-and-hands-work is not diversionary because it does not reduce our ability to concentrate on the other activity.

## Debilitating Recollections

One of the first rules for running a race is to never look back. It will break the runner's stride and rhythm; it may even cause him to stumble. "This one thing I do, forgetting those things which are behind, and reaching forth unto those things which are before" (Phil. 3:13, KJV).

Why does Paul make such a point of forgetting the past? Because it can be a hindrance to achieving our goals. There are two hangovers from the past which are handicaps; unfinished tasks and past mistakes. We feel guilty about both. We have left undone those things which we ought to have done, and we have done those things which we ought not to have done.

*Unfinished Tasks.* Our lives leave a trail of unanswered letters, unread journals, unread books, unvisited friends. These unfinished tasks nag at our subconscious and haunt us.

The mere sight of the morning mail, the unread memos, the list of unfinished jobs is often enough to paralyze us. Novelist Dorothy Canfield Fisher called it "anticipatory fatigue." We are overwhelmed by all that needs to be done, and it creates a fatigue which is just as real and debilitating as that resulting from actual work. A writer gazes vacantly at the blank page in his typewriter, sighing so audibly that you would think he'd just completed an 800-page book.

What can be done about the guilt of unfinished tasks? One answer is to form the habit of finishing what we begin, to be able to say with Paul, "I have fought the good fight, I have finished the course, I have kept the faith" (2 Tim. 4:7). One of the reasons Paul could forget what lay behind was that he was a finisher. He encouraged others to be finishers: "I want to suggest that you finish what you started to do a year ago. . . . Having started the ball rolling so enthusiastically, you should carry this project through to completion" (2 Cor. 8:10-11, LB).

Jesus observed, "For which one of you, when he wants to build a tower, does not first sit down and calculate the cost, to see if he has enough to complete it? Otherwise, when he has laid a foundation, and is not able to finish, all who observe it begin to ridicule him, saying, 'This man began to build and was not able to finish' " (Luke 14:28-30). A task half done is often as useless as a task never begun. It may be a momument to poor planning. In San Jose, California there is a complicated freeway interchange with a double overpass towering high above the freeway. The roads leading up to the interchange have never been completed and there are no plans to do so. Motorists grimace at the mute reminder of the misuse of public funds due to inept planning.

Good intentions and careful workmanship count for very little if the task is never completed. The engineer whose bridge *almost* spans the Mississippi, the homeowner who *almost* finishes the guest room, the housewife who *almost* bakes a cake long enough, and the sky diver who *almost* pulls the rip cord in time are all failures.

We must resist the temptation to start reading 10 different books before we've finished the first one. One way to "forget what lies behind" is to finish what we start. Leftover concerns about the first will hinder concentration on the other.

Some things from our pre-Christian lives, however, are better left undone. In Luke 9, Jesus called two men to be His disciples; "Follow Me," He challenged. Both gave an excuse which indicated other priorities. The first said, "Permit me first to go and bury my father" (v. 59)—obviously a delaying tactic. His father was not already dead or he would have been elsewhere making preparations for the funeral. He was saying, "I will follow you after my father has died, he is old and needs care." Jesus responded, "Allow the dead to bury their own dead; but as for you, go and proclaim everywhere the kingdom of God" (v. 60). There are some things which the spiritually dead can do as well as believers. We should not let unfinished tasks distract us from our spiritual calling.

The second said, "I will follow you, Lord; but *first* permit me to say good-bye to those at home" (v. 61). The man placed family ties and friends above his calling. Jesus responded, "No one, after putting his hand to the plow and looking back, is fit for the kingdom of God" (v. 62). Family ties and friendships can be distracting; driving a straight furrow while looking backward is impossible. It is as bad as a runner looking back. The ties and associations of our old life are better forgotten—that we may press on for the "prize of the upward call of God in Christ Jesus."

## Unresolved Guilt

*Sins of the Past.* Guilt associated with the sins of the past can also be debilitating. It can be like a millstone around our necks— slowing all progress in the Christian life. One young man, who came for counseling, felt He could never be used of God again because he had fallen into sin. He considered himself a "castaway" (1 Cor. 9:27, KJV)—disqualified from the race. Because he had blown it, he resigned himself to a place on the shelf for the rest of his life. As a result, he was severely depressed and even considered suicide.

In Psalm 32, David graphically pictures the effects of a guilty conscience on one's physical body. Unresolved guilt produces all kinds of psychosomatic illness. Some doctors have estimated that over one-half of their patients would be healed if they could be told with authority, "You are forgiven!"

We must deal with our past before we can experience freedom in the future. Satan is particularly adept at using our past to limit our future. He is called the "accuser of the brethren" in Revelation 12:10; he "accuses them before our God day and night." His objective is to immobilize by convincing us we have gone too far and that God cannot possibly forgive. Given our hopeless state, he suggests that repeating the sin will not make it worse. ("You might as well go all the way as often as you like.") He uses the guilt of past sins to create a *domino effect*—one fall encouraging another.

One young woman was active in God's service and was greatly used of God. One day, through a series of circumstances, she was led into sexual sin. Overwhelmed by her guilt, and realizing she could never recover her virginity, she felt she was disqualified from Christian service forever. Thinking that a new life of purity was impossible, she threw caution to the winds and gave up all resistance to temptation. Her promiscuous sexual relationships resulted in a pregnancy.

James Stalker, a Scottish preacher, said, "The great tempter of men has two lies with which he plies us at two different stages. Before we have fallen, he tells us that one fall does not matter; it is a trifle; we can easily recover ourselves again. After we have fallen, he tells us that it is hopeless; we are given over to sin, and need not attempt to rise."

One fall does matter. Even one sin causes us to lose something which can never be recovered. A valuable piece of china can be broken and mended, but it will never be the same again. One sin (crack) leads to another.

But to suggest that a new beginning is impossible is completely contrary to Scripture. Jeremiah observed the potter working at the wheel: "The vessel that he made of clay was marred ... so he made it again another vessel. ... Then the Word of the Lord came to me, saying, 'O house of Israel, cannot I do with you as this potter?' saith the Lord, 'Behold as the clay is in the potter's hand, so are ye in Mine hand, O house of Israel' " (Jer. 18:4-6, KJV).

The offer of a new beginning, however, does not negate the law of the harvest. We reap what we sow (Gal. 6:7-8). Brain damage from drugs is irreversible. David lost his son and suffered disastrous consequences in his family due to his sin of adultery with Bathsheba; nevertheless, he was forgiven and given a new beginning.

God offers total forgiveness, " 'Come now, and let us reason together,' saith the Lord: 'though your sins be as scarlet, they shall be as white as snow; though they be red like crimson, they shall

be as wool' " (Isa. 1:18, KJV). "For I will be merciful to their unrighteousness, and their sins and their iniquities will I remember
no more" (Heb. 8:12, KJV). God offers to clear the memory bank of
the computer so we can begin again with a clean slate. If God
forgets, why do we insist on remembering?

Our past need not control our future. The cycle of sin can be
broken. We can rise again, if we turn from our sin and accept
God's forgiveness. "If we confess our sins, He is faithful and just
to forgive us our sins, and to cleanse us from all unrighteousness"
(1 John 1:9, KJV).

Paul could have been debilitated by his past. He could have
been in constant remorse about his vendetta against Christians
before his conversion. He said, "I am the least of the apostles, who
am not fit to be called an apostle, because I persecuted the church
of God" (1 Cor. 15:9). But he dealt with the sins of the past at the
foot of the cross, "Forgetting what lies behind . . . I press on
toward the goal for the prize of the upward call of God in Christ
Jesus" (Phil. 3:13-14).

## Entangling Sins

There are not only sins of the past that must be dealt with and
forgotten, there are also sins of the present. "Let us also lay aside
every encumbrance, and *the sin which so easily entangles us*, and
let us run with endurance the race that is set before us" (Heb.
12:1).

We have already seen how diversionary activities and recollections of the past can be burdens which weigh us down in the race.
They impede progress toward our primary goals. They are like the
thorns which choke the seed with the cares, riches, and pleasures
of this life, so that it remains barren (Luke 8:14). They exhaust our
spiritual strength and cripple our activity for Christ.

We have also seen how the burden of unresolved guilt can
entangle us in further sin. Perhaps this is why Hebrews 12 links
the two. The entangling sin is spoken of in the singular, "*The* sin
which doth so easily beset us" (KJV). It is *the* sin to which we are
most vulnerable—perhaps a stubborn sinful habit (like sexual
lust, gluttony, or drunkenness).

It is hard to find more descriptive language for stubborn sinful habits which cling to us and entangle us. They may have been carried over from our pre-Christian lives or they may have begun as an innocent diversion. We have all experienced the cycle: (1) indulge in sin, (2) feel guilty, (3) resolve never to do it again, (4) experience victory, (5) fall again. Each time we repeat the cycle, our conscience becomes less sensitive (even seared); our resolve weakens, and the tentacles of habit hold us ever more tightly.

Jesus dramatized the cycle by telling the story of a man who had a demon cast out. The unclean spirit wandered to and fro seeking a new abode. Finding none, it decided to return to its original habitation. It was pleased to find the house unoccupied, swept, and put in order so it invited seven other spirits more evil than itself to go in and live there. "The last state of that man becomes worse than the first" (Luke 11:26). Renouncing sin is not enough. The man who was freed from the demon did not last because his life was left empty. Had he filled the vacuum with the indwelling presence of the Spirit of Christ, the story would have ended differently.

Seneca cried out, "Oh that a hand would come down from heaven and deliver me from my besetting sin!" He did not realize that God had already granted his wish. Jesus Christ, God's Son, has come down from heaven to deliver us from our besetting sins. "If therefore the Son shall make you free, you shall be free indeed" (John 8:36). He "is able to keep you from stumbling" (Jude 24).

If you are wondering why you can't seem to extricate yourself from the clutches of a stubborn sinful habit, it is because you are not under the control of the Holy Spirit. When Paul speaks of "redeeming the time," he adds, "And do not get drunk with wine, for that is dissipation, but be filled with the Spirit" (Eph. 5:18). In other words, place yourself under the control of the Spirit—not under the influence of alcoholic spirits.

The non-Christian seeks to overcome harmful habits by sheer willpower. For most of us, this is insufficient to break the chains of sin. "I see a different law in the members of my body, waging war against the law of my mind, and making me prisoner of the law of sin which is in my members. Wretched man that I am! Who will set me free from the body of this death? Thanks be to God through Jesus Christ our Lord! . . . For the law of the Spirit of life in Christ Jesus has set you free from the law of sin and of death" (Rom. 7:23-25; 8:2).

## Self-Discipline

Most of us have discovered that there is a big difference between knowing what to do and doing it. As we increase in our knowledge of the Scriptures, we seem to create a bigger and bigger gap between knowing what to do and what we actually do. We know the bridge across the gap is called *self-discipline*, but we can't seem to cross it. Peter says, "For this very reason, make every effort to add to your faith goodness; and to goodness, knowledge; and to knowledge, *self-control*" (2 Peter 1:5-6, NIV).

Self-discipline is the significant difference between winners and losers in the race of life. It is the difference between those who dream and those who achieve. If we aspire to anything great, we are only one step away. That step is self-discipline.

The wisdom of Solomon says, "A man without self-control is like a city broken into and left without walls" (Prov. 25:28, RSV). In ancient times, a city without walls was particularly vulnerable—it was without defense. It was prey to every kind of enemy—animal and human. The marauder was free to roam its streets, looting and plundering. Likewise, the man without self-control is vulnerable to every kind of satanic attack—to distraction and sin. He is without defense, a slave to his own passions and lust.

Though we speak of time management, in reality, time is not manageable. It is only possible to manage ourselves and our use of time. For this reason, self-discipline is crucial to the time-management process. What can be done to improve our self-control?

Galatians 5 says that self-control is a "fruit of the Spirit" for those who "walk by the Spirit" (under His control). In other words, if we place ourselves under His control, He works in us "both to will and to work for His good pleasure" (Phil. 2:13).

Men committed to Christ have been enabled to overcome severe obstacles through self-control. The Apostle Paul overcame his "thorn in the flesh" and wrote many of his epistles while in prison.

John Calvin (1509-1564) produced the greatest literary work to come out of The Reformation, *The Institutes of the Christian Religion* (1536), while suffering from constant headaches, spitting of blood, a hemorrhoidal vein (the pain of which increased to unbearable proportions because of an internal abscess that would not heal), intermittent fever, gallstones, kidney stones, stomach cramps, intestinal influenza, and arthritis.

Richard Baxter (1615-1691), a puritan theologian, published 128 books (more than 35 thousand printed pages) and was renowned for his house-to-house ministry in Kidderminster; yet he was a walking museum of pathological conditions. He wrote, "I have these 40 years been sensible of the sin of losing time; I could not spare an hour." He apologized for his books: "I wrote them in the crowd of all my other employments, in the midst of continual languishing and medicine, which would allow me no great leisure for polishing and exactness, or any ornament." Were men like Calvin and Baxter exceptional men, or were they ordinary men endowed with the fruit of the Spirit?

## Tools for Cultivating Self-Control

It is clear from Galatians 5 that the fruit of the Spirit needs to be cultivated. There are three tools which have been helpful to me in cultivating the fruit of self-control: mind renewal, making no provision for the flesh, and self-denial.

*Mind Renewal.* The most important principle in self-control is illustrated by the story of the man who had the demon cast out, only to be repossessed by eight demons (Luke 11). The man failed because he didn't understand the principle of "substitution." You can't overcome evil by simply renouncing it and casting it out. Something good must be substituted in its place. That is why Colossians 3 speaks of putting off the old man and putting on the new man; putting off anger, wrath, malice and putting on compassion, kindness, gentleness.

Suppose your besetting sin has to do with lustful thoughts. You get on your knees and ask God to take them away. You resolve you will not allow them to enter your mind. But the more determined you are not to think lustful thoughts, the stronger they become.

Try an experiment. Visualize pink elephants in your mind. Now exercise your willpower and stop thinking about pink elephants for 15 seconds. Were you able to do it? Of course not. Trying to push pink elephants out of your mind focuses your attention on more pink elephants. The only way to stop thinking about pink elephants is to think about something else—maybe red monkeys.

You can overcome lustful thoughts by focusing on what is pure and lovely. "Let your mind dwell on these things" (Phil. 4:8). The psalmist said, "Thy word have I hid in my heart that I might not sin against Thee" (Ps. 119:11, KJV).

The thought life is crucial in gaining mastery over self. In Proverbs 4:23 we read, "Be careful how you think; your life is shaped by your thoughts" (GNB). You aren't what you think you are, but what you think . . . you are! Paul speaks of "taking every thought captive to the obedience of Christ" (2 Cor. 10:5).

There are thousands of Christians who wonder why they are not getting any place in the Christian life. They wonder why they are crippled and impotent in their service for Christ. It is because the thoughts and imaginations of their minds have never been brought under the control of the Spirit of God. It is because they have not been transformed by the renewing of their minds (Rom. 12:2). "For the mind set on the flesh is death, but the mind set on the Spirit is life and peace" (Rom. 8:6).

*Make No Provision for the Flesh.* Jesus taught that "the spirit is willing, but the flesh is weak" (Matt. 26:41). Even though your spirit is controlled by the Spirit of God, the flesh is not to be trusted; therefore, "Put on the Lord Jesus Christ, and make no provision for the flesh in regard to its lusts" (Rom. 13:14).

I counseled a young man whose besetting sin was pornography. Pray as he would, try as he would, he could not get the victory. Then one day he told me he kept one lewd picture in his desk, just in case he was tempted! (He explained this would avoid the expense of a new girlie magazine if he fell!) I worked with an alcoholic who did the same thing with a small bottle of booze—

just in case he was tempted. That's making provision for the lusts of the flesh.

When Jesus dealt with lust, He suggested a shocking remedy. "If your right eye makes you stumble, tear it out, and throw it from you; for it is better for you that one of the parts of your body perish, than for your whole body to be thrown into hell" (Matt. 5:29). This radical surgery was necessary to cut off all opportunities for the lust of the eyes. Jesus was in favor of our burning our bridges behind us. In the case of pornography, He would have had a "burning-of-the-books." In the case of gluttony, "Put a knife to the throat, if thou be a man given to appetite" (Prov. 23:2, KJV).

When I am away on business trips, the greatest temptation is the TV set in the hotel room. It is distracting from other more profitable pursuits. I would really like to cut the cord, but at the very minimum I unplug it. Sometimes I have asked the maid to move it out, lest I make provision for the flesh.

Whether we are at home, at the office, or away, there are scores of diversions which beckon to the flesh. Because they are so available, we must remove them.

*Self-Denial.* In 1 Corinthians 9:25 we read, "Everyone who competes in the game goes into strict training" (NIV). The athlete's training rules eliminate anything harmful to the body. The program is designed to build his body, to improve his muscle tone, coordination, and endurance. More important, it is during training that the athlete gains the mastery over his body which permits top performance on the day of the race. Training is a period of self-denial; it takes willpower! And the key to willpower is want power. Because he wants the prize, he is willing to deprive himself.

Mark Spitz, who won seven gold medals in the Olympics, trained by swimming no less than eight hours every day from the time he was eight years old. He deprived himself of many of the pleasures of life, but he won the prize. The training paid off; Mark Spitz is now a millionaire!

Paul said it's no different in the Christian life: "I keep under my body and bring it into subjection lest that by any means, when I have preached to others, I myself should be a castaway" (1 Cor.

9:27, KJV). Paul felt that his bodily appetites must be under his control at all times. There is nothing intrinsically sinful about bodily appetites; it is perfectly normal to desire food, sex, sleep, and comfort, but they are to be in subjection and within the bounds prescribed by God. What did Paul mean when he said, "I buffet my body"? Apparently, he was referring to a voluntary discipline he inflicted on himself, probably by fasting or other physical privations.

In the *Book of Common Prayer* (collect for first Sunday in Lent), fasting is defined as "such abstinence that our flesh may be subdued to the Spirit." The value of fasting as an aid to subduing the body and mastering its appetites has always been recognized. *The Church of England Homily* (1562) says the first end of fasting is "to chastise the flesh, that it be not too wanton, but tamed and brought in subjection to the Spirit." It is often associated with prayer, and Jesus said there are some things which can be achieved only by prayer and fasting (Matt. 17:21; Mark 9:29).

The point is that we can gain more mastery over self if we purposely deprive ourselves of something we want. One of the most self-disciplined men I know makes a practice of denying himself something every day. One day it may be a meal; the next day it may be an hour of sleep, or the pleasure of a shower. He is bringing his body into subjection, and as a result he is disciplined in matters of the Spirit as well.

Jesus said, "If any man will come after Me, let him deny himself, and take up his cross daily, and follow Me" (Luke 9:23, KJV). Jesus deprived Himself, not only during the 40 days in the wilderness or the ordeal on the cross, but in everyday affairs. He missed lunch talking to the woman at the well, and explained, "My food is to do the will of Him who sent Me, and to accomplish His work" (John 4:34). Because of a full schedule during the day, preaching and healing, He deprived Himself of sleep at night in order to pray. And of course, His self-denial was *total* when He went to the cross.

It is this kind of self-denial that helps us focus and concentrate on the task at hand. No one can win the prize without self-denial. It means saying *no* to diversionary activities, making no provision for the flesh. It means control of the thought life, putting out of our minds the sins of the past. It means disciplined concentration on Jesus, the lead runner in the race, that we may escape the sin which so easily entangles us. It is the discipline of concentration.

# 12

# Murphy's Law and the Tyranny of the Urgent

A number of years ago, I was placed in charge of a division to launch a new product line for the company. It if proved successful, the venture promised higher pay, increased responsibility, and greater status—a major step forward in my career.

Initially, my staff was small. We could not afford to hire additional people until the sales began to come in. It was a tremendous challenge to launch a new business venture on a shoe string, and I welcomed it, but we were all overworked as a result.

I began to spend more and more time at the office both in the evenings and on weekends. It was the opportunity of a lifetime, and I wanted to give it my best. My wife seemed to understand, though later she confessed to crying a lot during that time. I was with the children less. My devotional life began to suffer. I still preached occasionally, but the power seemed to be missing.

The gradual deterioration of my spiritual life was imperceptible at first. Eventually, it manifested itself in selfishness, irritation, and criticism. I kidded myself into thinking that since God had provided the opportunity, He wanted me to give it my all. Ironically, the very reason I accepted the job, to give glory to God, became less important than personal success.

There is an old saying, "You can't kill a frog by dropping him in boiling water." He reacts so quickly to the sudden change in temperature that he jumps out before he's hurt. If you put him in cold water and warm him up gradually, he doesn't jump until it's too late and he's cooked. In retrospect, I should have decided to jump earlier. The change in my spiritual life and in my family life was so gradual, I didn't realize the danger. The Lord was gracious; He snatched me out before I was "cooked."

After two years, the company decided to dispense with my division. The sales were increasing rapidly, but we were still unprofitable. Another company wanted to buy the division, and as is often the case in a takeover, new management was installed. I saw everything I had worked hard for dismantled. The situation was beyond my control, and the glorious opportunity was shattered. I was plunged into the pit of depression, not realizing that God was at work. I resigned to take another job on the West Coast.

At the time, the whole thing seemed tragic, but it took this disaster for God to get through to me. I began to realize the vanity of any pursuit without God. "Unless the Lord builds the house, they labor in vain who build it; unless the Lord guards the city, the watchman keeps awake in vain. It is vain for you to rise up early, to retire late, to eat the bread of painful labors; for He gives to His beloved even in his sleep" (Ps. 127:1-2). In retrospect, I found I had been laying up for myself treasures on earth, which alas ... were stolen by thieves (Matt. 6:19). I had neglected the true treasures in heaven. I had tried to serve two masters, found it impossible, and wound up serving the wrong one. The kingdom of God and His righteousness were no longer first in my life, so all these things were taken away from me. How ironic that I had to relearn the lesson (Matt. 6:33) that had ushered me into the kingdom some 16 years before.

How did it happen? What was it that cut the moorings and allowed me to drift so far from shore? It happened so subtly; it was so unintentional and yet insidious. If God had not intervened, would I have drifted into the rapids, past the point of no return and over the falls?

It happened because I allowed the urgent to crowd out the important. I rationalized: The job was so urgent, my regular quiet time could wait. The project was due on Monday; I could go to church any time. The business clients were in town only this week, my family would be there next week and the next. We had to get the business off the ground in two years, I had the rest of my life to build for eternity. The urgent crowded out the important. It is what Charles Hummel calls "the tyranny of the urgent" (*Tyranny of the Urgent*, InterVarsity).

## The Urgent vs the Important

General Eisenhower once explained to his officers that there is an inverse relationship between what is important and what is merely urgent. The more important, the less likely it is urgent; the more urgent, the less likely it is important. The general arranged his desk with two in-boxes: one marked *urgent*, the other marked *important*.

Important things are those which contribute significantly to our goals. They tend to have long-range consequences. Urgent matters generally have only short-range consequences. They may or may not contribute to our goals. Most frequently they do not. Important things seldom need to be done today, or even this week. Louis Halle laments the tyranny of the urgent in world affairs: "One of the reasons for the rarity of statesmanship is that, in a world increasingly rushed to death, the long-range waits on the immediate. What is urgent takes priority over what is merely important, so that what is important will be attended to only when it becomes urgent, which may be too late."

The tyranny of the urgent in the family is bewailed by a western song which speaks of a father who had no time for his growing son. When his boy wanted him to play ball, he never had time. In later years, when the father wanted to visit, his grown-up son was too busy. It occurred to the father that his son was like he had been. He'd grown up like his dad. Too late the father realized that the urgent had taken priority over the important.

We live in constant tension between the urgent and the important. At work we become firefighters, troubleshooters, crisis managers. We are so busy fighting fires we have no time to plan for tomorrow. Ironically, this guarantees that we will have more fires tomorrow; it is a vicious cycle that feeds on itself. But as one of

my associates quipped, "When you're up to your neck in alliga-
tors, it doesn't help much to say we ought to drain the swamp!"

The insistent ringing of a telephone is urgent in the minds of
most people. As a result, they take their calls as they come in. I
was in a busy department store where five customers were lined
up waiting to make a purchase. When the phone rang, the busy
clerk promptly left all her customers standing there with money
in hand to answer the phone. Before she finally hung up, three
customers became so disgruntled, they dropped their intended
purchases and walked away.

A man's home used to be his castle. It offered seclusion and
protection from the urgent crises of the business world. It was at
home that the important got done—time with God and family.
Today the telephone breaches the walls of seclusion with invitations, demands, and idle chatter. Our family takes the phone off
the hook during mealtimes to avoid these interruptions.

Further, business matters tend to spill over into our home and
church life. Overtime at the office prevents me from having supper with my family. The emergency meeting at work keeps me
from attending our small-group Bible study. An early-morning
phone call keeps me from having my quiet time. The tyranny of
the urgent frustrates every goal we hold sacred.

## What's Really Important?

Is there any escape from the tyranny of the urgent? The key to
freedom lies in distinguishing between what's really important
and what's merely urgent. The new Japanese version of Philippians 1:10 renders Paul's prayer: "That you may discern what is
important." This is the crucial issue. To choose between right and
wrong is not difficult, but to choose between two good alterna-
tives is not always easy. We can spend far too much time on some
things, and far too little on others. The difference between the
disorganized person on the edge of a breakdown and the calm,
unflappable type is often that the second has determined what is
important. He does not waste time, anxiety, or energy on the
unimportant.

Now pull out your *time inventory* and ask what was really

important and what was only urgent. Figure 5 can be helpful in analyzing the activities recorded on your *time inventory*.

Cell 1 includes those activities which are both important and urgent. We tend to call these *crises*. Most of us could do with fewer of these. On the job, such examples would include the breakdown of important production equipment or the threat of losing a major customer. Off the job, Cell 1 might include an automobile accident or the sudden illness of a family member. In the church, examples include crisis counseling (e.g., suicide threat, marital breakup, or restoring a fallen brother). Of course we attend to the matters in Cell 1 immediately because they are not only urgent, they are very important. They have top priority.

Cell 2 includes items that are important, but not urgent. These items should really be second on our priority list, but they are often postponed because they aren't urgent. Examples include planning, training, Bible study, prayer, and time with the family. We spend far too little time on the items in Cell 2.

The activities in Cell 3 often consume 50 to 70 percent of our time. They are urgent, but they contribute relatively little to our goals. Telephone calls are a prime example. If you keep a record of all the phone calls you receive over a period of time, you will find only a small proportion are really important. Drop-in visitors are another example. Many come simply to kill time; they have

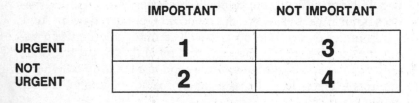

Figure 5

nothing important on their minds. They do not even consider their visit urgent, but their presence demands immediate attention. The epitome of all items in Cell 3 is my dog who barks urgently to come in or go out. She can't seem to decide where she would rather be. As a result, we open the door for her 10 or more times every evening—only to silence her incessant barking.

I would like to believe that Cell 4 does not exist. Items here are neither urgent nor important. Yet, a typical *time inventory* will probably reveal 10 to 40 percent of your time spent in this cell. Trips to the coffee machine, socializing, TV viewing, and other time killers are examples.

If we take the time to sort out our daily activities into the important/urgent matrix, we can add up the percentage of our time spent on important affairs and those not so important. It will also indicate where we can find additional time to apply to our goals. But let's be honest; most of us believe that virtually every- thing we do is important. This is simply not true.

While attempting to reallocate activities, it will be helpful to remember the *80/20 rule* (80 percent of the results we achieve come from 20 percent of the things we do). Items which fall into Cell 2 (important, but not urgent) are probably part of the 20 percent that contribute 80 percent to our results. One man, recov- ering from a heart attack, returned to his job on a part-time basis (spending only three or four hours a day at work). He was shielded from crises by his associates and quickly discovered he could achieve virtually the same results in three hours that had previ- ously taken eight hours. He was able to do this because he spent those hours on only the most important activities.

You will probably also discover that 80 percent of your time is spent in the *not-important* column. If this is the case, you are either undisciplined or a victim of the tyranny of the urgent.

Ask yourself what is really important. If you're not committed to spending at least 10 minutes a day on one of your primary goals, it's probably not really that important to you. If Jesus felt time with His heavenly Father was so important that He must say *no* to other demands on His time, shouldn't we?

If Nehemiah felt building the wall was so important that he

couldn't afford to interrupt for an urgent meeting with Sanballat and Geshem (Neh. 6:3), perhaps we should look more critically at the meetings we're asked to attend. Neither Nehemiah nor Jesus were afraid to say *no* to escape the tyranny of the urgent.

One woman who attended my seminar decided the time she spent every morning washing and putting up her hair was relatively unimportant. She adopted a more manageable hairstyle which gave her an extra 30 minutes every morning. She used this time to increase her quiet time from 15 to 45 minutes. The extra 30 minutes in the Word and in prayer began to change her life. She approached her job with a different attitude. After a month, her boss noticed the change and promoted her to a more responsible position. She was also able to tell him what made the difference.

One man came to me expressing his frustration with the Christian life. He wanted to serve the Lord, but didn't seem to be equipped. I asked him how much time he was spending in the Word of God and found it less than one hour per week. I also found out he carried a briefcase full of "urgent work" home every night. I suggested he relegate this "urgent work" to the office, and spend his time at home with his family and in the Word of God. He was able to carve out one hour every evening for Bible study. Things began to happen in his life. Within three months, he had started a neighborhood Bible study in his home. He found the Lord enabled Him to work more efficiently at the office and to finish that "urgent work." "Seek ye first the kingdom of God, and His righteousness, and all these shall be added unto you" (Matt. 6:33, KJV).

## Scheduling around Murphy's Law

Perhaps the most frustrating thing about schedules is how often they must be canceled due to some unforeseen crisis which is both important as well as urgent (Cell 1). This is particularly unnerving to engineers and scientists like myself. We would prefer to think of life as predictable and controllable. One of the major endeavors of science, beginning with Newton, has been to formulate laws which describe natural phenomena with mathematical precision. But the unpredictability of the stream of events in our lives continues to elude us. As someone has said, "The only thing you can count on is your fingers." It is this unpredictability which one day inspired Murphy to postulate his now famous law: "If anything can go wrong, it will!"

The success of Murphy's law has inspired many corollaries and other postulates. The first was a simple ammendment: "If anything can go wrong, it will . . . and at the worst possible moment!" Then O'Toole came out with his now famous commentary on Murphy's Law: "Murphy was an optimist!" Here are 20 corollaries:

- When you've come to the conclusion that things can't possibly get any worse you will be proven wrong.
- Negative expectations yield negative results. Positive expectations yield negative results.
- When things are going well, expect something to explode, erode, collapse or disappear.
- Once a job is fouled up, anything done to improve it will only make it worse.
- Every man has a scheme that will not work.
- All things being equal, you are bound to lose.
- Everything costs more than you first estimated.
- If you tinker with something long enough, eventually it will break.
- Left to themselves, things always go from bad to worse.
- If there is a possibility of several things going wrong, the one that will go wrong is the one that will do the most damage.
- If everything seems to be going well, you have obviously overlooked something.
- Nothing is as easy as it looks.
- Everything takes longer than you expect.
- The other line moves faster.
- An object will fall so as to do the most damage.
- The chance of bread falling with the buttered side down is directly proportional to the cost of the carpet.
- All warranties expire upon payment of money.
- The first 90 percent of the task takes 90 percent of the time, and the last 10 percent takes the other 90 percent.

- The more time you have to do a job right, the more likely you are to goof it up.
- Anything good in life is either illegal, immoral, or fattening.

How do we manage to remain sane with these laws constantly working against us? Why do things go wrong? Isn't it because we live in a fallen world? Murphy's law is really just a restatement of the curse in Genesis 3:17-18: "Cursed is the ground because of you; in toil you shall eat of it all the days of your life. Both thorns and thistles it shall grow for you."

The Christian does not deny Murphy's law anymore than he denies the Fall, but his perspective is different. He knows that God is in control and that He can overrule. He has the promise: "We know that God causes all things to work together for good to those who love God, to those who are called according to His purpose" (Rom. 8:28). We Christians, like everybody else, find that the desired event didn't happen *when* we needed it. What we wanted wasn't *where* we wanted it. The thing produced was not *what* we wanted. We didn't know *how* to do it or we did it incorrectly. We find ourselves in such predicaments, and yet we have assurance that God can work all of this together to bring about good.

Our first reaction to the unforeseen crises that foul up our schedules is irritation and resentment. Sometimes we are overwhelmed; the day seems to run out of control. But James says Murphy's law should cause us to rejoice: "When all kinds of trials . . . crowd into your lives . . . don't resent them as intruders, but welcome them as friends!" (1:2, PH.) because God is aiming at something we can't see.

Joseph must have known Brother Murphy pretty well. His brothers mistreated him and sold him into slavery. His master's wife tried to seduce him. Those he helped and befriended in prison forgot him and neglected to return the favors. But God was at work! By the time Joseph next met his brothers, they were starving while he was second in command over all of Egypt. Joseph could say to his brothers, "You meant evil against me, but God meant it for good" (Gen. 50:20, RSV).

## Our Plans May Not Be God's Plans

There is danger of a schedule becoming an idol, so sacred it can't be altered. Henry Kissinger, while he was secretary of state, said, "There can't be a crisis next week. There's no time in my schedule!" If we feel our schedule is cast in concrete and get irritated when something comes along to interfere with it, we have in effect cut ourselves off from the guidance of God. Sometimes *our* plans are not God's plans. Sometimes we are so stubborn that the only way God can get through to us is with a crisis. "It is pleasant to see plans develop. That is why fools refuse to give them up even when they are wrong" (Prov. 13:19, LB).

When my job in Massachusetts began to fall apart, it seemed like a catastrophe. I could see nothing good in it. My plans were shattered. I was so depressed I couldn't see the hand of God in those events. I was even mad at God for allowing the crisis to interfere with my schedule. I was unaware of the "time of my visitation." Subsequent events have proven over and over that the crisis of those days was intended to work together for good in my life. My ministry was saved; it expanded, and became more fruitful. My new job was better for me and my family. And the geographical location (California) was an added plus. It took a painful crisis to shake me loose from a plan I clung to tenaciously.

Planning and scheduling must be done with the sovereignty of God always in view. "Now listen, you who say, 'Today or tomorrow we will go to this or that city, spend a year there, carry on business and make money.' Why, you do not even know what will happen tomorrow. What is your life? You are a mist that appears for a little while and then vanishes. Instead, you ought to say, 'If it is the Lord's will, we will live and do this or that.' " (James 4:13-15, NIV). Even the apostles made their plans subject to God's will: "I will return to you again *if* God wills" (Acts 18:21).

Being willing to die to our plans is the only way to bring forth fruit. Being willing to lose our plans is the only way to find His plans. "The mind of man plans his way, but the Lord directs his steps" (Prov. 16:9). If we have given our time to God, we can be confident that He controls crises and interruptions.

The Chinese ideogram for crisis contains two characters meaning *danger* and *opportunity*. (See Figure 6.) If a people rooted in the fatalism of Buddhism can believe that, surely Christians should—believing as we do that God can transform evil events into good.

Yet, if we were thrown into prison as Paul was, would we see the opportunity he saw? The dejected Philippians must have been encouraged to get Paul's viewpoint, "Now I want you to know, brethren, that my circumstances have turned out for the greater progress of the Gospel, so that my imprisonment in the cause of Christ has become well-known throughout the whole praetorian guard" (Phil. 1:12-13). Paul did not complain about being chained to a guard 24 hours a day. Instead, he thanked God for the captive audience. The rotation of guard duty every 6 hours permitted evangelizing the whole guard unit—one man at a time. Paul seized his crisis as an opportunity. He "made the most of his time" even though the days were evil.

But how can we make the most of the hidden opportunities in crises? We need to plan for the unexpected. We need to program time into our schedules to accommodate Mr. Murphy.

A competent general draws up the battle plan before he engages the enemy, but he also has contingency plans to allow for unforeseen events. Similarly, God had a perfect plan for an obedient Adam and Eve, but He also had a contingency plan "written from the foundation of the world" (Rev. 13:8) which involved a Second Adam (1 Cor. 15:45-48).

Contingency plans in military operations involve the concept of "strategic reserve." The same concept may be applied in scheduling. The biggest mistake people make in scheduling is to allocate every minute of their day. This approach is guaranteed to fail; there are just too many unexpected interruptions. Leaving a "strategic reserve" open for the unexpected will enable us to meet crises without jeopardizing our overall schedule.

How much reserve should we allow? There is no definite answer to this question. Ideally, we should commit no more than 50 to 75 percent of our time to planned activities, leaving the remaining 25 to 50 percent open. For example, if we spend 8 hours at work, we should probably leave 4 of those hours unscheduled to absorb unexpected events.

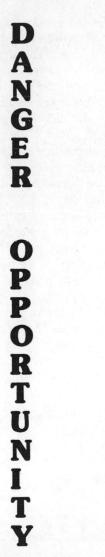

"CRISIS"

Figure 6

When should we schedule the reserve? Consider the scheduling patterns in Figure 7.

The *block pattern* is generally the best. All work is scheduled during prime time. If it takes longer than expected (due to interruptions or bad judgment), we can continue working in the afternoon. If things work out according to schedule, we have a large block of unscheduled time available in the afternoon. With the other patterns, even when things work out well, the gained time is scattered throughout the day. This makes it difficult to start a new task.

On the other hand, if work involves appointments, as in a medical practice or counseling, it is best to allow *reserve time* between appointments in case they take longer than expected.

Remember Parkinson's Law: "Work expands to fill the time available for its accomplishment." Scheduling *reserve time* can be counterproductive if we always use it to finish up the preceding task; therefore, we should always have a contingency plan prepared for those days when Mr. Murphy is on vacation. Perhaps we can get a head start on tomorrow's *to-do list* or refer to an *opportunity list* of activities to fill the spaces with.

One of the most amusing examples of scheduling around Murphy's law involves two busy mothers in Austin, Texas. They were driving their children to school one morning when they collided. Both got out and inspected the damage but decided they really didn't have time to have an accident then. They agreed to meet

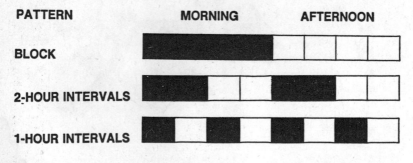

Figure 7

later (during their *reserve time,* I suppose). That afternoon, each woman drove to the scene of the accident, carefully maneuvered her automobile into the exact position of the accident, and then called the police. "Don't let the urgent crowd out the important."

## Scheduling around People

Whenever we deal with people, we are bound to encounter the unexpected. Most of our interruptions are related to people (e.g., drop-in-visitors and telephone calls). They interrupt our train of thought and delay our schedule. For this reason, most time-management books suggest ways of minimizing our contact with people. The impression is left that good time managers work in places inaccessible to others or have a closed-door policy. They let their secretaries take all calls and return only the most important. They use clever phrases or gimmicks to cut inopportune visits short. In effect, they barricade themselves from other people.

In chapter 7, we discussed the problem of time bandits, people who rob us of the intended use of our time. Jesus Himself often said *no* to people because of higher priorities (usually with other people). He instructed His disciples to avoid socializing and accepting too much hospitality for the greater priority of preaching the Gospel.

But Jesus also said *yes* to people not on His schedule. He said *yes* to Jairus and quickly accompanied him to heal his dying daughter (Mark 5:22-43). On the way, he stopped to heal a woman who had been hermorrhaging. How could a woman with a menstrual problem take precedence over a little girl in the clutches of death? Ironically, while Jesus dealt with the woman, a messenger came saying it was too late; Jairus' daughter had died. But Jesus went on to raise her from the dead.

When Jesus heard of the beheading of John the Baptist, "He withdrew from there in a boat to a lonely place by Himself" (Matt. 14:13). The multitudes followed and would not leave Him alone. In this instance, He did not shut the door; He "felt compassion for them, and healed their sick" (v. 14). When it was evening, He had the perfect excuse. In fact, it was the disciples who suggested that He send the multitudes away to get food. But Jesus said, "They do not need to go away" (v. 16) and He fed them with five loaves and two fish. Finally, after they were fed and satisfied, Jesus retreated to the mountain to pray alone, as He had originally intended.

Sometimes the disciples tried to shield Him from interruptions. "And they began bringing children to Him, so that He might touch them; and the disciples rebuked them. But when Jesus saw this, He was indignant and said to them 'Permit the children to come to Me; do not hinder them; for the kingdom of God belongs to such as these' " (Mark 10:13-14).

Sometimes Jesus said *no* and so must we. But at other times, He paused to take up a little child, to heal, or to feed a hungry multitude. How did Jesus know when to say *yes* and when to say *no*? He explained, "I pass no judgment without consulting the Father. I judge as I am told. And My judgment is absolutely fair and just, for it is according to the will of God who sent Me and is not merely My own" (John 5:30, LB). For every decision He prayerfully waited for His Father's instruction. He had no divinely-drawn blueprint; He discerned the Father's will moment by moment in a life of unceasing prayer. By this means He warded off the urgent and accomplished the important.

One thing is clear about Jesus's priorities: people always came before schedules. Schedules will pass away; people last for eternity. In the Parable of the Good Samaritan (Luke 10:30-37), Jesus contrasted a priest and a Levite, who had no time to help a man half-dead in the ditch, with a despised Samaritan who took time. The Samaritan administered first aid, carried him to an inn, and made the necessary arrangements for his care (at his own expense). The priest and Levite were too concerned about their schedules. Jesus applauded the Samaritan and said, "Go and do the same" (Luke 10:37). He applauds us when we put people ahead of schedules.

Dying to a schedule to give people priority is not always easy. It may mean canceling an appointment with the hairdresser to go and pray with a friend in crisis. It could mean putting aside sermon preparation Saturday night to minister to a troubled brother. It may require canceling an appointment with a client to talk with an office colleague going through divorce.

The next time a person interrupts you, think not of your work and your deadlines. Instead, think of that person's needs. Is it an opportunity to "bear one another's burdens, and thus fulfill the Law of Christ?" (Gal. 6:2) Is it a chance to become their servant for Jesus' sake? Perhaps it's an opportunity to share Christ. "Conduct yourselves with wisdom toward outsiders, making the most of the opportunity . . . that you may know how you should respond to each person" (Col. 4:5-6).

Put yourself in the other person's shoes. How often have you talked with someone on the telephone who was in a hurry; they seemed to want to get on with more important business? Or perhaps you've had an appointment and been ushered in and out of the office by the clock. You didn't enjoy it, because it reduced you to "nonimportance." You felt like a walking interruption.

> Executives are hard to see,
> Their costly time I may not waste.
> I make appointments nervously,
> And talk to them in haste.
> But anytime of night or day,
> In places suitable or odd,
> I seek and get without delay
> An interview with God.
> Author Unknown

When a person interrupts, we should be flattered that he has chosen us to spend time with, that he values our friendship and our words. "Be humble, thinking of others as better than yourself. Don't just think about your own affairs, but be interested in others too, and in what they are doing" (Phil. 2:3-4, LB).

It is possible to be so scheduled, that we have no real friends. Friendship is a sphere in which Christians should excel, but we cannot organize a friendship by the clock. It takes time—when time is not. A friendship usually develops in three stages: comradeship, companionship, and communication. Each of these words begins with *com*, the Latin for "together."

Comradeship, from *camarade*, literally means "together in the same chamber or room." Friendship begins by spending time together. Common experiences and circumstances are the seeds of a friendship. But planting these seeds takes time.

Companionship, from *companio*, literally means "taking bread together." Doing things together builds a friendship. Whether playing tennis or refinishing old furniture, shared activities help us to know and like each other.

Communication, from *communicare*, means to "make common" or "make known." Talking together about our feelings and opinions so that we understand and know each other deepens a friendship. Open communication cannot be forced; it takes time to unfold.

The Bible has a great deal to say about interpersonal relationships. Jesus said that loving God and people is what it's all about. But most of us experience very few deep, personal relationships. We don't have the time. Yet we take the time for TV, shopping, and all manner of other impersonal activities. When will we schedule time for people? When will we take time to know and be known by another person?

If this book has left you with the idea that "redeeming the time" means using every moment, rushing hither and yon, pushing people out of the way to get on with the job, I have failed. As stated in the Preface, "The goal of this book is not to make you a time nut, but to help you accomplish all that God wants you to do—with a relaxed peace and joy."

I personally have been interested in better management of my time to allow more time for God and people. It is the GAP method of time management found in Ephesians 5:15-17 which makes it possible to finish our work in less time to create a *strategic reserve* of time—mostly for people.

Without *goals* and *priorities* we will never escape the tyranny of the urgent. If we do not have our eyes fixed on a goal, the urgent will crowd out the important.

*Analysis* of our time inventory tells how much time we're spending with God and with people. It's shocking to see how many urgent things interfere with more important times with God or family.

It is only by planning and scheduling that we can make time for people and for God. There should be specific times set aside for prayer, for family, and for friends. But there should also be a *strategic reserve* for unexpected opportunities to meet the needs of others.

May God give us grace to escape the tyranny of the urgent. "If the Son makes you free, you will be free indeed" (John 8:36, RSV).

# Epilogue
# The Finished Life

We have marveled at the closing statement of Jesus' life, "I have finished the work which Thou gavest Me to do" (John 17:4, KJV). From the beginning of Jesus' ministry, His goals were clear: (1) to preach good news to the poor, (2) to proclaim release to the captives, (3) to proclaim the recovery of sight to the blind, (4) to set free those who are downtrodden, and (5) to proclaim the favorable year of the Lord (Luke 4:18-19). How could He use the word *finished* when so many remained untouched? For each one who found forgiveness and a new life, thousands were still in the chains of sin. For each blind man who had his sight restored, there were hundreds who still walked in darkness. How could He say *finished* when He had just started?

Yet on that last night, realizing full well the urgent needs still unmet, the Lord Jesus had peace; He knew He had finished God's work. In a short life of 30 years, with no more hours in the day than we have, He accomplished all that His Father had given to Him to do. What was His secret?

I do not fear death. What I fear is that I should end before I finish—or not finish well. (Few, they tell me, finish well.) But if some prophet were to tell me my time was up, I would, like Hezekiah, pray for more time to finish. Hezekiah's prayer was answered, but after 15 more years, could he say, "It is finished"?

What made the difference between Hezekiah and Jesus? Was it not Jesus' ability to distinguish between the urgent and the important? He was told that it was urgent that He go to the sick bed of Lazarus, but He knew it was more important to delay and raise him from the dead. They said it was urgent to heal the sick and dying at Capernaum, but He said it was more important to go on to the next town. Jairus said his daughter's case was urgent (her time was running out); yet Jesus stopped to heal the woman with a hemorrhage. He was unhurried and unfrenzied because He refused to let the urgent crowd out the important. He could distinguish between the two because He spent time with His Father; He got His marching orders from Him.

If you set your eyes on Jesus and follow Him to the finish line, your life can be "finished" as well. Jesus said some startling things about the Christian's potential for accomplishment. "I say to you, he who believes in Me will also do the works that I do, and greater works than these will he do, because I go to the Father" (John 14:12, RSV). D. L. Moody's life was changed when Henry Varley said to him, "Moody, the world has yet to see what God will do with a man fully consecrated to Him." Most of us don't even come close to realizing that potential; the missing ingredient is faith.

The word for "belief" in the Greek assumes a great deal more than mere intellectual assent. It implies total commitment and dependence on Christ. This kind of faith responds to a passage such as Ephesians 5:15-17 in obedience. This kind of faith not only believes that God has a purpose for our lives, it earnestly seeks to "understand what the will of the Lord is" in every detail. It not only believes that God can work good out of evil, it sets out to "make the most of the time." It not only believes that the Holy Spirit can direct our steps, it is careful to plan ahead under His direction—"walking wisely."

This book is not finished; it remains for you to write the last chapter. If the book has anything to commend it, it will be found in that final chapter. The best commendation is a changed life. When the Apostle Paul spoke of letters of commendation, he said, "You are our letter, written in our hearts, known and read by all men . . . written not with ink, but with the Spirit of the living God, not on tablets of stone, but on tablets of human hearts" (2 Cor. 3:2-3).

What will you say in that last chapter? Will your life show more organization, more time for people, and freedom from frenzy? Will you begin by taking inventory and setting goals? Perhaps you've never even tried a *to-do list*. What *one thing* will you do to change your life—to escape from the tyranny of the urgent?

Perhaps the biggest stumbling block to change is the belief that we are unchangeable. You may feel you are a hopeless case— completely disorganized and out of control. Christ invites you to place total trust in Him as the new manager of your life. The Bible promises, "If any man be in Christ, he is a new creature; old things are passed away; behold, all things are become new" (2 Cor. 5:17, KJV). Do you believe He can change you?

# My Pacesetter

The Lord is my pacesetter,
  I shall not rush.
    He makes me to stop
      for quiet intervals.
He provides me with images of stillness
  which restore my serenity.
He leads me in ways of efficiency
  through calmness of mind,
    and His guidance
      is peace.
Even though I have a great many things
  to accomplish each day,
    I will not fret
      for His presence is here.
His timelessness,
  His all-importance
    will keep me in balance.
He prepares refreshment
  in the midst of my activity
    by anointing my mind
      with His oil of tranquility.
My cup of joyous energy overflows.
  Surely harmony and effectiveness
    shall be the fruit of my hours,
And I shall walk
  in the pace of the Lord
    and dwell in His house
      forever.

                         Author Unknown